short, sharp
and snippy

Also by Megan Dougherty

Quilting Isn't Funny

short, sharp and snippy

more cutting-edge quilt humor by
Megan Dougherty

The following pieces first appeared, some with slightly different wording, formats, or titles, in *Generation Q* magazine: "The Contest," "10 Tips For Dating a Quilter," "A Few Words About Your Quilting By Your Cat," "Attn: Marge," "Bye-Bye Laws," "How to Quilt: A Tutorial By Mom," "My Acceptance Speech," "The Annual Self-Curated Quilt Show," "Thank You For Calling," and "The New Rules."

The following pieces first appeared, some with slightly different wording, formats, or titles on the Badass Quilters Society website at www.BadassQuiltersSociety.com: "Letting Go," "Meet the Candidates," "Quilting Reality Shows," "Things You Need To Stop Doing (To Be a Better Quilter) By People You Know," "Quilt the Pounds Away," and "A Few Words About Your Quilting By Your Dog."

The following pieces first appeared, some with slightly different wording, formats, or titles, on The Bitchy Stitcher blog at www.TheBitchyStitcher.com: "Have Yourself A Merry Little Festive Midwinter Thing," "How Pickles Make Quilting All Better," "Super Helpful Amazon Reviews," "Antonio," and "The Minimalist Quilt Studio."

All other pieces appear here for the first time.

Publisher: Megan Dougherty
Cover design, and interior design and layout by Megan Dougherty

For David & Miles & Devon

contents

introduction

As a semi-professional writer, I am highly skilled at procrastination. For example, just today, as I was sitting down to write this introduction, I managed to waste a good 20 minutes by Googling, "why are introductions necessary," "does a book really need an introduction," "how to convince someone to write your introduction for you," "introductions for dummies," and "George Clooney divorce rumors." Not only do I know far more than I ever wanted about my imaginary boyfriend's clearly sham marriage, I also know a great deal more about the purpose and scope of book introductions. Or a great deal less, depending on how you look at it.

According to various websites that are without question written by authoritative experts, there are several things that a good book introduction should accomplish or contain. For instance there should be words, punctuation, and hopefully a lick or two of sense, which is more than can be said for a lot of the websites I looked at today. I also learned that if you are going to tell readers why they should read the book, that should go in the foreword and should be written by somebody who is not the author and is ideally somebody famous. Now, I do know a few famous quilters, in the sense that I know who they are and could probably pick them out in a lineup if called upon to do so, and none of them were willing to write a foreword for me. So, if you are desperately wondering why you should read this book, I'm afraid you're on your own with that one.

If what you are really looking for is how this book came to be, well apparently that belongs in a preface, not an introduction, and it is supposed to "add credibility" to the book and author. I'm not sure how knowing that I came up with most of the ideas for the pieces in this book after throwing myself to the floor and whining for several hours until it was easier to get up and write something than stay down there adds credibility, but okay. To be honest, I think my credibility comes from the fact that I've been quilting and writing jokes about it for ten years now and I have heroically managed to make the vast majority of those jokes *not* about the size of my stash, my inability to restrain myself in a fabric store, or my husband's ire at my profligate fabric spending. I have written about zombies, the Buddha, cats, dogs, art critics, fashion, minimalism, dating, weight loss, home decor, reality shows, fabric design, etiquette, urban legends, your mom, my mom, wills, insurance, sex (often refered to as "shenanigans"), and pickles—and managed to relate all of that to quilting in some way or another. There's not that many other quilt humor writers out there who can say that. There's not that many other quilt humor writers out there at all, really, but my point still stands.

I am also told by various bloggers—sorry, *experts*—that any explanation of why I wrote the book should also be contained in a preface, not an introduction. If I were to write a preface, which I am obviously not doing at all, and were to give some accounting of why I decided to tackle the inherent absurdity of quilting in a second volume, I would probably say that the world we are living in right now is an incredibly scary place, and I'm pretty sure that if we are going to survive it with our sanity intact, we are going to need to laugh about something—

and it might as well be quilting. If I am honest, I would also say that I made some pretty good bank on my first book, and mama needs a Florida vacay like yesterday, but mostly it's the bringing-laughter-into-a-frightening-and-uncertain-world thing.

Another thing I have read about introductions is that intros and prefaces are almost the same thing and that most people just use the word "introduction" because something called a "preface" sounds stuffy and academic and people tend to skip over it. I guess "introduction" sounds friendly, like you think book and reader might hit it off so you invite them both to the same party and then subtly herd them both over to the dessert table at the same time so you can say, "Hey, reader! Have you met my book? You both like jokes about copyright infringement and weird smells in fabric!"

So, if that is the basic purpose of an introduction, and it sounds as good as any, then Dear Reader, allow me to introduce my book, *Short, Sharp and Snippy*, a collection of brief, humorous pieces about quilting, written between 2012 and 2018. Those were not easy years for me, as in that time period I lost my brother and my mother to cancer, had three major surgeries—with complications!—and struggled daily with depression and self-doubt. I do not personally recommend any of those things if you are thinking about writing your own quilting humor book, because believe it or not, they don't really help much. What does help, though, is having an amazing family of smart, funny weirdos to keep you laughing even when you think you don't want to, and a loyal cadre of readers who tell you they will read every word you write, even the sad ones that are not quilting-related at all. You all are still the stuffing in my trapunto, and I thank you for coming along on this crazy decade-long ride with me.

the
contest

Just a couple years after I started quilting (and writing about it) every-body started getting all litigious. Or at least threatening to get litigious. I'm not sure anyone ever actually sued anybody else for copyright infringement but a lot of nasty letters have certainly been emailed, I do know that.

I figured somebody out there was probably pretty sick of so many people threatening to get Judge Judy involved, and might get a wee bit defensive about it on occasion. Particularly if it's a beleaguered quilt shop owner running a contest and trying to keep everyone from ogling her boyfriend.

Oh, and it should be noted here that I worked pretty hard to come up with a good name for a quilt shop that wasn't already in use. I liked Clever Notions so much, I ended up using it for the name of my online shop.

Thank you for entering The Clever Notions 2012 Quilt Design Contest. This is the second year of our competition, but not the second consecutive year, because I was distracted throughout most of 2011 by an unfortunate lawsuit. The terms of the settlement say that I cannot reveal the names of the parties involved, so let's just call them Shmeryl Shmonson and Shmindy Shmith. Unfortunately, I am also not allowed to discuss the details of the suit or the settlement, so let's just say that we're going to have to be a little stricter about the rules this year so that Shmeryl and Shmindy don't get an itch to lawyer up again.

Eligibility:

The Clever Notions 2012 Design Contest is open to anyone over the age of 18 who has never published a quilt design and who has never said anything nasty about me on Facebook. I'm sorry, but you know who you are, and I know who you are (Shmynthia) and there's really no need to pretend that I would do anything except "accidentally" spill my coffee all over your entry form.

Entrants must be citizens of the U.S. or Canada and must register in person at the Clever Notions Quilt Shop. At the time of registration, entrants must provide a picture I.D., a current credit report, at least three character references from non-family members, and a plate of brownies. All entrants are required to sign a very lengthy and complicated legal document that basically says you agree not to hold me or the The Clever Notions Quilt Shop responsible if somebody sees your design and thinks that it kinda looks like that quilt she made five years ago which everybody with eyes can see is just a rip-off of a Gwen Marston quilt from, like, forever ago, but which she apparently thinks is so original she'll probably try to sue Gwen retroactively for future copyright infringement. So, in other words, if somebody says you're a big ol' copycat, it's not my fault and you can't try to drag me in. I've got lawyers now, too, you know. Big, scary lawyers.

Employees and family members of The Clever Notions Quilt shop are not eligible to compete and neither is anybody I catch flirting with Hank Fowler, owner of Hank's Hardware. Or maybe I should call him Shmank. Shmank and I will be getting married very soon, despite what Shmank says, and I simply cannot be expected to remain objective about quilts submitted by people who think it's okay to horn in on another woman's boyfriend. If you think I'm kidding, go stop in Shmank's store and take a good look at his biceps. Guns like that do not come along every day, and if I do what I have to do in order to keep them in my possession, well, who could blame me? And don't think you can go in there and bat your mascara at him without me knowing about it. I have ways.

Categories:

Quilt designs will be accepted in the following categories:

• **Baby quilts.** These must be no larger than 42" x 42" and must only use solids, blenders, and prints that are intended for children. Anybody who sends in a baby quilt using one of those Alexander Henry prints with the half-naked hunky guys will be disqualified. And I'll be keeping the quilt.

• **Appliqué.** Quilts submitted in the appliqué category must use appliqué as the primary design element. Turned edge and fused appliqué with stitched edges are acceptable, but raw edge appliqué is out because that's just lazy.

• **Traditional patchwork.** These quilts will employ traditional blocks in new and interesting ways. Please note that anybody can pair up a Churn Dash with a Pinwheel and it is not a violation of your copyright if you once did that too and stamped the word "Copyright" all over the blog tutorial you wrote for it. A "c" in a circle is not a magic talisman, people. Did I mention the big, scary lawyers?

• **Modern.** I am very, very excited to include modern quilting in this year's competition. To qualify, all you have to do is add the word "modern" to the name of your quilt. Isn't that easy? Scores will be weighted towards quilts that use mostly white and grey and the first quilt that comes in using only white and grey automatically wins.

Look, a lawyer! Did I scare you? Good.

Judging:

All entries will be judged by me and possibly Shmank if he's not too worn out that day, if you know what I mean. (From doing bicep curls—what did you think I meant?) I will carefully rate each quilt based on workmanship, originality, execution, and whether the creator has tried to sue me lately. Points will be deducted if the creator has tried to sue me and has also written me sugary-sweet letters about how we should "put all this behind us" and "act like sisters again." Mom and Dad are on my side, Shmindy. I hope you know that.

Prizes:

Third place: A stack of fat quarters, and a coupon for 10% off any purchase of $75 or more at The Clever Notions Quilt Shop.

Second place: A slightly bigger stack of fat quarters and a coupon for 15% off any purchase of $75 or more at The Clever Notions Quilt Shop.

First place: An almost new, top-of-the-line Bernina sewing machine that may or may not have come into my possession as part of a settlement for a frivolous lawsuit. It has "Shmeryl and Shmindy's Quilt Pattern Company" painted on the side, but I'm pretty sure I can cover that over with some flames or skulls or something. In addition, the winner will receive a free one-hour consultation with a paralegal from the firm of Venkman, Stantz and Spengler and my permission to touch Shmank's biceps for 30 seconds. (It's longer than you think—time kind of slows down when you get near them.)

This contest is void where prohibited by law. The Clever Notions Quilt Shop reserves the right to change these rules at any time without advance notice. But I'll tell you right now, if I get even the tiniest whiff of a lawsuit, I'm taking Shmank off the table.

10 tips for dating a quilter

I don't really know what it's like to date a quilter since I've been married forever. And since I married, like, the third guy I ever dated, I don't really know that much about dating either, to be honest. But I do know a lot about lists.

Let's face it: not everyone can be lucky enough to date a quilter, but there's no doubt that it's everyone's fantasy. Who hasn't dreamed about walking into an office party or a violent sporting event with a sweet piece of quilter candy on his or her arm? But not so fast there, hotshot. There are things you should know about dating a quilter, so read through these handy tips before you decide to commit.

1. Know that you may spend a lot of nights alone. Unless you have somehow managed to snag a superquilter (a quilter who makes a decent living from quilting—very rare), your quilter is going to have a day job, leaving him only nights and weekends to quilt. When faced with the choice between fondling you or the new Alison Glass fat quarter bundle he just scored on sale, the fabric may very well win. But don't be discouraged. Use his fabric fetish to your advantage and you can become the lover of his dreams. Hint: he loves fabric cut into long strips; imagine the possibilities.

2. Realize her quilts come first. You are just a drone with a middle management office job and a softball league on Saturdays. She, however, is a committed artist and you need to respect her need to create. So if she blows off your league championship game to finish up some UFOs, just remember that whiny boyfriends don't get quilts for Christmas.

3. Be prepared for fabric distraction. Does your quilter seem to have a short attention span? Does he look everywhere except deep into your eyes? He's probably just found something cloth-based that he's now imagining in a quilt block or on a binding. Everything from the linen napkins at the restaurant to the velvet curtains at the movie theater can draw his attention, so remember to bedeck yourself with colorful fabrics to keep him focused on you. Try pairing up an Anna

Maria Horner scarf with a Melody Miller skirt. And if he ever catches a glimpse of your Jay McCarroll undies? Score!

4. Remember: She is *a* quilter, not *your* quilter. Yes everybody needs warm covers for their beds and sofas, but just because you bought him a nice steak dinner, you're not entitled to free quilts. If you really want to win his heart, ask him to make a quilt on commission and offer way more than the going rate. Most likely, he'll end up giving you the quilt, but still be prepared to pay, because quilters are generally broke and desperate for cash.

5. Be on the lookout for guys who want to steal your quilter away. So, you've managed to overcome your personal shortcomings and have successfully convinced that hunky longarmer to date you. Don't get complacent! Remember that every guy he meets is a potential rival, so be prepared to q-block them at any moment.

6. Learn how to romance a quilter properly. Flowers. Candlelight. Long walks on the beach, holding hands, at sunset. Yes, you can try all of those things, and they might work, but if you really want to make a quilter swoon, tell her you're related to Carolyn Friedlander and she sometimes sends you fabric samples. Sure, it may not be true, but you won't be able to pry that quilter off you with a crowbar, so who cares?

7. Spot red flags. Take a good look at what your quilter makes before you decide to woo her and make her yours. Are her quilts all roughly 36" by 54"? Are they mostly made of cat hair? Are they all art quilts with titles like "Men Suck," "I Really, Really Hate Dudes," "Death to All Penis-Having Humans," or "I Really Want A Baby, Like, Right This Minute, But Barring That I'll Just Own 18 Cats and By The Way Men Suck"? If yes, proceed with caution.

8. Stop obsessing about your ex. Don't drive a new quilter away by constantly comparing him to the last quilter you dated. It's great that your ex was a "free-motion machine" and could "quilt it all night long," but you need to appreciate the quilter who's right in front of you and save your praise for him. Delete your ex's number from your phone and stop checking his "hand work" board on Pinterest.

9. Spot a quilter who can't commit. Just how many UFOs does she have in her closet? Are there baskets of half-stitched embroidery projects and partially completed knitting shoved into the corners? Has she ever taken you fabric shopping only to walk out of the quilt store empty handed? Sure, we've all done a little casual quilting from time to time, but a quilter who can never settle down with one project is probably never going to make you that Storm at Sea quilt you've been dreaming of. Or marry you.

10. Never ask about their "number." Even in today's semi-enlightened society, there is still stigma attached to the notion of "too many" quilts. Even though you may be "quilt-positive", there are still people out there who will call a quilter "fast" and "easy" just because he's addicted to making quilts that are, well, fast and easy. Never, ever ask, "So, just how many quilts have you made anyway?" if you want to keep your quilter from running away in embarrassment. Just check her Instagram account; they're all there for the world to see anyway.

a few words about
your quilting
by your cat

Quilters do love their cats, but my question has always been, do their cats love them back? Oh, sure it may seem like they do, but you know they're just trolling for treats. Before I started quilting, I had a cat who would sit on my chest at 5:30 am every morning and stare at me until I opened my eyes. And as soon as I did he would slowly turn his head to the side, nip me on the nose, and then jump down to go wait in the kitchen for his break-fast, which he would not consume unless I sat next to him while he ate it. This one's for you, T.J.

Oh, hey. How you doing? I didn't notice you staring at me and repeatedly trying to shove my very ample body off your sewing chair. I thought you weren't using it anymore. Yes, I know you were still sitting in it at the time. Your thighs are very cushy and clearly become an integral part of the chair when you sit. We've discussed this.

Well, now that I have no choice but to be awake, can I ask if you're going to thread your machine now? I'm not saying that I care one way or the other if you do. I was just wondering. Are you going to use that thread? That pretty pink one? With the end just dangling down and swinging like some sort of prey animal I've never actually encountered but I am pretty sure moves exactly that way? Hey, do me a favor and hold your arm just like that so I can sink my back claws into your leg and…POUNCE!

CRASH!

Oh wow. That didn't end up the way I imagined it. How did I get so fat anyway? I'm pretty sure that's your fault. You may not be aware of this, but cats don't really need thighs as cushy as yours. Oh, and by the way, I'm all done with the appetizer you put in my food bowl this morning and I'm ready for the main course now.

I couldn't help but notice you tidied up in here recently. I'm trying to remember, but I can't seem to recall giving my permission for that. You usually have some nice fabric piles for me to roll around in; could you put some back, please? No, not scraps! This isn't Soviet Russia, for Pete's sake. Some nice freshly cut ones that you intend to use in your next quilt. No, I don't know what the difference is—don't ask me questions about the nature of the universe before breakfast.

Oh, hey—I see you have your laptop on. This would be the perfect time for me to lie across the keyboard while we discuss your internet habits. I want you to know that your Pinterest board, "Kitteez I Luuv," offends me deeply. Why do you have to spend your time looking at pictures of other cats, cats with extra-fluffy fur who fit into tiny little boxes? You know those big eyes are Photoshopped, right? I just think this is giving you unrealistic expectations about what cats are supposed to look like and how they act when you put stupid hats on them. You come anywhere near me with a hat, and you're losing a hand, let's just get that clear right now. Anyway, I really want you to stop looking at kitty pics online. I should be enough cat for you. More than enough, really. Speaking of which, are you ever getting my breakfast, or do I have to climb on top of the refrigerator and knock the Friskies onto the floor again?

Now that we have that out of the way, I need to find that quilt you just finished. The one that's a gift for your dearest friend in the whole world, who just got married or birthed a litter or something. You made her an extra-special quilt with all that Tula Pink fabric you've been hoarding for years and years. That one. Where is it? I neeeed it. I need it RIGHT NOW. WHERE IS THAT QUILT, SO HELP ME, WOMAN, I WILL—oh, there it is! Let me just get right on the middle of it and...

YAAAAAAARK!

Ah, that's better. Forgot to tell you I escaped for a while this morning when the man human brought the morning paper in, and do you know what I found? Right in the yard? A perfectly good dead bird. It was very tasty. Look, see? There's a feather!

Oh, stop whining. It wasn't a very good quilt anyway. And that's really what I heaved myself in here to talk to you about. See, your quilts are just boring. So many flowers and polka dots and swirly things that represent nothing I can eat or pee on. You need to make a quilt that reflects my essence, my soul. Because, let's face it, I am the center of your entire universe and if I am not pleased I will just bite your toes while you and the man human are doing that thing you sometimes do in the bed that doesn't involve me. Oh, you're right; I do that anyway. I guess I'm not pleased, am I?

So, here's what I think you should do: Gather up all those bird fabrics you collected. Cut out a bunch of birds. Fuse them all over some green fabric, all belly up, and then stitch little Xs over their eyes. ISN'T THAT BRILLIANT? I call it *The Fanciest Feast*.

Why don't you get started on that—after you get my breakfast and, what the heck, a handful of treats, too; I deserve it—and then I'll come back in and help you. I'm pretty sure that pointy thing that goes up and down when you sew gets in your way, so I'll swat at it for you. No need to thank me. Just add some cheese and leftover tuna to my breakfast and we'll call it even.

attn: marge

I recently got a straight-stitch Juki sewing machine, and I was relieved to see that the manual was only a few pages long, unlike the hefty tomes that came with a couple of my other machines. I know there is an art and a skill to writing things like sewing machine manuals, but I do wonder if the people who have to write them would like to let their creativity loose once in a while.

Congratulations on your purchase of our machine! You must be a very educated, savvy, and, let's be honest, darn sexy consumer to have purchased the most technologically advanced sewing machine since, well, since the last one we made. We want to be sure you completely enjoy your sewing experience, so please take this manual and a nice cappuccino or an iced latté and sit down in a quiet corner and read it over very carefully. Failure to read the manual thoroughly or to do so without an appropriate beverage could void your warranty.

For safe operation:

1. Keep your eye on the needle while sewing. Do not look at the hand wheel. Do not look at the fabric the cat is chewing on. Do not look at the small child who is about to swallow a handful of straight pins. Look at the needle. See the needle? See it go up and down? Up and down. Uuuuup and dooooown. That's right. Keep looking at it. You are getting very sleepy. You will desperately desire a new machine in approximately six months. Preferably the model we're going to release just after you void your warranty with that can of Diet Coke.

2. Remember to turn off the power switch and unplug the cord when:

> • You are done sewing.
> • You are not done sewing, but you are taking a break to have another iced latte.
> • You think you might be done, but you're not sure, so you scoot your chair back a couple inches.
> • The hot UPS man comes to deliver a package and you need to go lie down with a cold cloth on your head to recover.
> • Changing the needle.
> • Changing the thread.
> • Changing the bobbin.

- Changing your shoes.
- During a thunderstorm.
- During a power failure.
- On odd days during a leap year.

3. Do not use the foot controller as a launch pad for Matchbox cars

4. Do not plug the machine into an extension cord. Unless it's one of those really expensive ones.

For a longer service life:

1. Avoid direct sunlight. Do not get the machine wet. And, whatever you do, do NOT feed it after midnight.

2. When cleaning the case, use only a neutral detergent and a soft cloth. Do not lick your thumb and try to rub that spot off. It won't damage the case; it's just gross.

3. Do not hit the machine. Do not kick the machine. Do not take your machine to the nearest overpass and drop it into rush hour traffic. Do not travel into Mordor with your machine and hurl it into the fires of Mount Doom. You can, however, strap it to the next Soyuz rocket headed to the International Space Station, because that would be freaking awesome.

In the event that your machine needs service or repair, you will need to find an Authorized Repair Center. To locate an Authorized Repair Center, you must call our Repair Center Hotline. To find the number for the Repair Center Hotline, you must visit our Repair Center Hotline website. To get the URL for our Repair Center Hotline website, send a self-addressed stamped envelope to our Corporate Offices in Montana, not the other ones in Delaware. Be sure to write ATTN: MARGE in really big letters on the front and back of the envelope. You should probably slip a twenty in there, too, just to be sure.

Turning your machine on and off:

Before you attempt to turn on your machine, please observe the following precautions:

1. Please use only regular household electricity when powering this machine. Do not attempt to hook this machine up to a huge series of galvanic cells that your kid made for a science fair project. It's also probably best if you don't ask us how we know this is a bad idea.

2. When plugging in the machine, grasp the plug firmly and push straight into the socket. Oh, wait! You have to make sure it's off first! Sorry!

3. If electric shock occurs as a result of not turning the machine off first, you may void your warranty.

4. Do not allow the power cord to be bent, cut, pulled, twisted, modified, mollified, mollycoddled, hornswoggled or flimflammed.

5. When the power cord is not in use, wrap it gently in pure silk and place it gently on a soft cushion, preferably one made from real goose down, not that synthetic stuff that Ikea keep trying to convince you is just as good. You might also sing to it softly—it likes Celine Dion and Abba.

When you are ready to turn on the machine, take several deep, cleansing breaths until you feel relaxed and focused. Clear your mind of all thoughts. Do not think about cheese. Do not think about those odd charges on your husband's credit card bill. Do not think about the UPS man. Okay, think about the UPS man for, like a minute, but then stop. When you have emptied your mind and you are at one with the universe, slowly extend your index finger, and gently press the power switch until it is in the "on" position.

Now, quickly turn it off again, unplug the power cord, and go lie down for a while. You don't want to take these things too fast. Maybe you should have another latte and think about the UPS man some more. Failure to think about the UPS man could void your warranty.

bye-bye-laws

I have written a lot about guilds, despite never having joined one, but I did go as a guest with a friend once, and that pretty much did it for me. The highlight of that meeting was the guild president talking about all the things that volunteers were needed for, and then looking increasingly ticked off as absolutely no one volunteered for anything. I assume she eventually managed to rope a few people into doing something, but I don't know if it involved physical threats or blackmail or both. I do know that every group I have ever been involved with in any capacity always has a number of people I like to call The Aggrieved Ones. Somebody is always doing those poor people wrong, and they love to let you know about it. My fictional guild has a whole lot of Aggrieved Ones, and I suspect many real ones do too.

Dear Members,

At the last general meeting, the president proposed a small change to one of our by-laws, namely an increase from two to three in the number of meetings a non-member may attend before he or she is required to pay membership dues. While there was little objection to the change and the measure passed easily, it seems the notion that they could be changed at all inspired a large number of our membership to come up with ways to "improve" the by-laws even further.

Below you will find a list of the proposed amendments and additions. Please read them thoroughly and come prepared to vote at the next general meeting. Please understand that if any of these proposals pass, the entire elected board will resign en masse and form a new guild that has no by-laws at all, just a guild drinking song, a secret handshake, and a list of people to be banned from the new guild forever and ever.

Proposed Changes to the Sew Sassy Stitchers By-Laws:

1. This is Donna Milhouse here, the one you all call the "Crazy Ferret Lady," and yes I do know about that. I may lurk in the corner and just knit ferret hats during meetings, but I'm not deaf. If there is already a by-law forbidding ferrets at meetings then I think we should change it so that I don't have to leave all my sweet, furry boo-boos at home. If I leave them alone too long they start eating their little hats.

2. That we add something that says no one is allowed to emit any sort of bodily gas during meetings. If I can't wear my new Joan Collins Diamond Shoulderpads perfume because some people have a "sensitivity" to nice smells, I shouldn't have to be subjected to the end result of your chili cheese dog dinner.

3. There should be a by-law that says whoever stole my favorite seam ripper needs to give it back RIGHT NOW.

4. I think we should make Tom Hiddleston our guild mascot and change our name to the Hiddle-stitchers.

5. And seam ripper stealers should get no refreshments ever and have to sit in the back row next to the Crazy Ferret Lady whenever the good speakers come.

6. Breath mints. 'Nuff said.

7. There should be a law against hogging the good parking spot.

8. I think we should be able to touch the quilts at the quilt show. For as long as we want. With our feet.

9. If someone's favorite seam ripper goes missing during a meeting, we should be able to do cavity searches on everybody until it turns up.

10. Can we start having meetings at Applebee's? My boyfriend's the assistant manager there and he can get us all half-price appletinis with the purchase of any full-size entrée.

11. Since a seam ripper thief is running rampant throughout meetings, grabbing other people's precious tools and hiding them who knows where, and nobody seems to care that lawlessness and hooliganism are now the norm at Sew Sassy Stitchers gatherings, I propose that we bring in a band of big, muscle-bound bikers to stand all around the room and glare at anyone who even looks like she might be thinking of putting her grubby mitts anywhere near my seam ripper. And if they actually catch someone in the act of absconding with my beloved

tool, they can cart her off to their biker clubhouse or wherever they go when they are up to no good and I do not care what they do with her. I bought that seam ripper on Amazon with a gift card my cousin Brenda gave me for my birthday and it is irreplaceable.

12. If people insist on dumping out their supplies all over the table and then one of those supplies rolls off the table and lands in someone's lap, I think that person should get to keep what lands in her personal space. I scored a good seam ripper that way.

how to quilt:
a tutorial by your mom

As I mentioned in my first book, my "mom" character is one that people constantly assume is based on my real mom. Actually, the character is just an excuse to put "your mom" in the title of things because I always giggle like an idiot over that.

Step 1. The first thing you need to do is get a decent sewing machine. I know you're perfectly happy with that plastic contraption with all the buttons and lights and Twitter feeds you bought at Target, but I still think you should take my old Singer treadle machine. It only has four moving parts and weighs more than your husband. Did he get that Jenny Craig brochure I sent him, by the way?

Step 2. Sit up straight. Honestly, you make me tired just looking at you.

Step 3. Choose a pattern. I'm going to tell you right now I will not help you make anything "wonky." Wonky is what you get when you keep the HBO on while you're sewing and get distracted by all the naked people.

Step 4. Choose your fabric. I can see already that you're going to insist on all those bright colors and fabrics that don't even have prints on them, but surely all that tangerine can't be good for your eyes, dear. Look, I have all these lovely muddy browns and baby poop greens. Nice soothing colors that won't burn holes in your retina.

Step 5. Thread your machine. Go ahead. I'll just wait over here while you flip through that 600-page manual. Is there anything on HBO right now?

Step 6. Check your scant quarter-inch seam. Accuracy is everything, my dear, and so instead of relying on that cheap quarter-inch foot you bought on Amazon, we're going to check your seams the old-fashioned way: with a grad student from MIT and a mass spectrometer.

Step 7. Cut your fabric. See this? This is not a rotary cutter. This is a fingertip amputation system, and it works great. So you should just go ahead and lop off the ends of all your digits now because you're gonna do it eventually anyway. While you're on the phone with the emergency dispatcher, I'll just be tracing 300 squares with this extremely faint fabric marker and cutting them out individually with huge scissors.

Step 8. Pin your fabric. Let's see, for about two and a half inches of fabric we're going to need roughly 37 pins. You can never have too many pins, just like you can never have too many grandchildren. Not that I would know. Oh, and don't hold pins in your mouth. Charlene sent me a link to a story about a woman who accidentally swallowed a pin and it worked its way through her whole body, poking all her organs and it eventually lodged in her ovary and she never gave her mother any grandchildren.

Step 9. Sew. As long as you don't think you could fit a couple more pins in there, go ahead and place your fabric under the foot and start sewing. Now, despite what all the bloggers do, you should try to actually sew in a straight line. Charlene's daughter loves to say, "It doesn't matter; it's MY quilt!" But let me tell you there's not a longarmer between here and Dubuque that will touch one of her quilts and that's because they're so wavy you could hide a small child in the pleats.

Step 10: Once you have the quilt top all put together, you need to make the backing. No, you can't just use a bed sheet. Yes, I'm sure fifty cents for a queen-sized bed sheet from the bargain bin at the thrift shop is a great deal, but for all you know people did stuff on that sheet. What do you mean, what stuff? Stuff. Please don't make me say it out loud; you know I get hives.

Step 11: Make your quilt sandwich. There are two ways to secure your backing and batting to the quilt top: pinning and spraying copious amounts of some toxic substance all over the quilt, the floor, yourself, and most likely the cat. Ever tried to bathe a sticky cat? Not fun. Besides, I'm pretty sure all those chemicals can't be good for your aging ovaries, so you might as well get down here on the floor with me and start pinning. Wear knee pads.

Step 12: Quilt your sandwich. This is not really as hard as it looks. Just put on the special foot, drop the feed dogs, attach the custom made flat bed extension, adjust your thread tension, hook up the bulk of the quilt to the pulley system you have installed in the ceiling over your machine, adjust your thread tension again, put on gloves, reattach the quilt to the pulley system after it falls off, throw back a bracing shot of whiskey and GO! No, I meant start quilting. Come back here!

Step 13: Bind your quilt. Look, I know all the cool kids are finishing their binding by machine and they're all perfectly happy with it, but have you ever looked at one up close? It looks like they did it while their hair was on fire. I am going to show you how to do it by hand with stitches so tiny they may not actually exist in this dimension. I call it Quantum Quilting. Don't look at me like that. I watch *The Big Bang Theory* every week—something's bound to rub off.

There, now! Aren't you proud of yourself? If you want, maybe next week I can teach you how to cook or vacuum or dress yourself like an actual grown-up. Where are you going? Is there something good on HBO now? Stand up straight, sweetie!

the red carpet

I love the inane pageantry of award shows and award show red carpet coverage. I think that kind of grandiosity ought to be applied to every award ceremony ever, including Most Improved Handwriting at elementary school graduation and Chamber of Commerce Businessperson of the Month.

Hello, and welcome to E! News coverage of the 14th Annual Sew Sassy Stitchers Quilt Show red carpet. All the local quilting stars are here—and let me tell you, they have outdone themselves this year—and we're here to focus on all the fabulous fashions. And look! Here comes Marge Sullivan, whose quilt, *I Don't Know, Just A Thing I Made Up* is in the running for Best in Show this year! Marge, tell us about what you're wearing.

Marge: Oh, well, this is a t-shirt I saw on Facebook and just had to have. It says "I Only Need Three Things: My Cat, My Quilts, And A Large Stack Of Harlequin Romances, Preferably The Ones Where Someone Falls In Love While They're Pregnant, I Really Dig Those For Some Reason." See, it has a sewing machine on it!

E! News: And so many fonts!

Marge: At least thirty!

E! News: And tell us about your quilt. How was it to work in improv for the first time?

Marge: Well, I'll tell you, I thought it was pretty strange since I'm so used to being told what to do, but once I realized that unbridled freedom could be its own straitjacket, I kinda got into it!

E! News: And it shows. Good luck tonight, Marge. And here we have Sarah Peterson; her quilt, *I See You Copying Me*, is nominated tonight in the Small Appliqué category. Sarah, who are you wearing?

Sarah: Well, this top is from Target. Or maybe Old Navy, I can never remember. And these leggings are from some multi-level marketing scheme my neighbor Junie is doing, Rola Rooter, or something.

E! News: And tell us about these fabulous earrings.

Sarah: Oh, yes, I make these myself and I sell them in my Etsy shop. They're made from the lint I clean out of my sewing machine!

E! News: And is that cat hair I see in there as well?

Sarah: Yes, thank you for noticing!

E! News: Congratulations on your nomination this year. This quilt seems like a departure for you; tell us about that.

Sarah: Yes, normally I only make quilts that are from free patterns I find on the internet, but so many other people were doing the exact same thing every year, I got tired of being everyone's inspiration. I mean, get your own ideas, right? So, this year, I just appliquéd a big NO onto a white background. Let's see them try to copy that!

E! News: Definitely a bold statement. Good luck! Oh, now we have a treat for you, ladies and gentlemen. Here comes Don Cornetto, and if I'm not mistaken, Don has made every single thing he's wearing. Is that right, Don?

Don: That is absolutely correct, and as you can see, it is a veritable riot of colors and flavors and smells.

E! News? Smells?

Don: Yes, my pants are made from strips of scented fabric! I've got chocolate, grape, coconut, pine forest, spring rain, and gym locker! Would you like to take a whiff?

E! News: Oh, we could smell you coming, Don! Congratulations on your recent appointment to the guild board as Donation Coordinator. Will you be bringing your unique sense of style into this role?

Don: Oh, absolutely, especially since I have a LOT of this scented fabric leftover. Also, I plan to choose our monthly charity quilt recipients via a dance-off and I will be storing all the donated fabric and batting in the trunk of my car—and let me tell you, it is a VERY attractive car.

E! News: Thank you, Don, and enjoy your evening. And let's see if we can get a word with one of the biggest stars of the evening, Lucinda Dickson, who once had a quilt pattern published in *Country Quilter's Bi-Monthly* magazine back in the late eighties. Lucinda, who are you wearing?

Lucinda: Issac Mizrahi.

E! News: THE Issac Mizrahi? Did you work directly with him on this design?

Lucinda: Yes, we spoke at length over the phone when I placed my QVC order. He said, and I quote, "My dear, you are going to love the 4-way stretch on these knit denim Bermuda shorts, and this cold-shoulder, bell-sleeve, plaid lace top is simply to die for." Honestly, I won't let anyone but Issac dress me. He simply knows a woman's body so intimately.

E! News: Now, you are being honored as the Featured Quilter of this year's show. Tell us a little about that.

Lucinda: Well, usually this just a bone they throw to the non-famous quilters to help shore up their self-esteem, but this year the guild board decided to pay homage to someone with actual accomplishments. I think I speak for the entire guild membership when I say, "Finally."

E! News: And will we be seeing your famous quilt, *Scrappy Rail Fence*?

Lucinda: Oh, yes, though that was the name used in the magazine; it will be shown here under its actual title, *Majestic Dreamways of the Purple Panjandrum*.

E! News: Well, I'm sure everyone is very excited about the chance to meet you and rub elbows with a real live quilt celebrity.

Lucinda: I will be suing anyone who tries to rub my elbows for assault and copyright infringement.

E! News: Right. Well, that's all from the red carpet. Stay tuned for our live coverage of the awards ceremony, followed by *Kwilting With the Kardashians*!

my acceptance speech

Naturally, all these newly elevated award ceremonies should allow ample time for acceptance speeches, including the part where the recipient shouts their litany of thank-yous over the orchestra trying to get them off the stage so that there's a hope of ending the festivities before midnight.

Oh! Oh my gosh! Oh, I just can't believe this. Well, I *can* believe it, but I'm just so surprised. I never in a million years thought that my little quilt would win Best In Show! I thought the one I made last year was going to win; I mean, I slaved over that thing for a year. And this one? Took me a couple weeks, tops. Honestly, when I get home, I'm taking this ribbon and hanging it on last year's quilt. You know what won last year? Something with a whole bunch of gray in it. Like that's even a color.

There are so many people I need to thank. First let me thank Kelly, Arlene, Mavis, Jennifer, and Cynthia—my fellow nominees. Thank you, Kelly, for not ripping out that one little spot in the corner where your machine skipped three stitches. Thank you, Arlene, for using all that gray; apparently, the judges are as over it as I am. Thank you, Mavis, for showing up at the nominees' luncheon completely plastered and falling face down in a potted plant, singing Bon Jovi into the dirt. I don't think this had any influence on your loss; I just want to thank you for it. A Blaze of Glory indeed. And thank you, especially, Jennifer and Cynthia, for getting so many people to bet against me in the guild pool. You just paid for me and my best girl, Trina, to go get deeply meaningful quilt block tattoos in unmentionable places.

Well, now that I'm up here at this podium, I don't intend to sit down anytime too soon, so who else can I thank? I'd like to thank the maker of my sewing machine. I'm not going to name any brand names, because that would constitute an endorsement, and there needs to be some cha-ching-ching first. No, I mean the actual person who assembled my machine, because I'm pretty sure you left your chewing gum somewhere inside it. That thing seizes up if a cloud passes over or someone burps in the next room, which is why I ended up making a quilt that looks like I was kidding. Oh, did you think I made those blocks wonky on purpose? This isn't modern quilting, people; it's frustrated quilting.

I'd also like to thank my husband, Carl. Carl has apparently decided that if he hovers long enough in the doorway of my sewing room staring at me and sighing, I will abandon my quilting efforts and come "watch *The Simpsons*" with him. Yes, I used air quotes around "watch *The Simpsons*." That's Carl's code for getting up to marital shenanigans. Honestly, if I didn't have Carl giving me an excuse to, um, release my frustrations with that damn machine every once in a while, there would no longer be a machine. Just a bunch of unidentifiable mechanical bits embedded in the walls.

I'd like to thank the person who invented Pepperidge Farm Double Chocolate Milano cookies. That individual is so dear to my heart, he (or she, makes no difference) is pretty much welcome to come over and watch *The Simpsons* with me anytime.

And naturally, I want to thank my bestie, Trina. Thank you, babe, for all the laughs, the tears, and the absurdly strong mojitos you made that one time. Thank you for talking me down when I went out on the roof with my chewing gum-infested sewing machine and threatened to drop it on the concrete patio. Thank you for creating that Pinterest board full of men in kilts. Thank you for listening when I went through that little phase where I thought I'd never want to watch *The Simpsons* again and thank you for lending me that book. Yes, that one. No, I'm not done with it yet.

Oh, right. Ahem. I can't forget the lovely people at Fabripalooza, my one-stop shop for all my quilting and crafting needs. Conveniently located in Tower Plaza, just off the I-99/370 split, their helpful staff and wide selection always help me fulfill my creative fantasies. It's a festival of fun at Fabripalooza! Be sure and ask them about their quilt show sponsorship program.

I'd like to thank one last but very special person: me. That's right; I said me. If there was one person without whom I could not have created this quilt, it's yours truly and frankly, everybody else was just in the way. So I thank me for learning how to quilt, for being really darn good at it, and for not going on some sort of rampage when that thing that looked like what you dump out of a vacuum cleaner canister won last year. In fact, I think I should get a separate award just for that. Or at least some Milano cookies.

the annual
self-curated
quilt show

I'm (probably) never going to enter any of my quilts into an actual quilt show, not even the ones that are internet-based. My entire Instagram feed is basically my own personal quilt show, and I show everything, even the Cheeto crumbs and the blocks sewn in upside down. And the chin zits.

Welcome to the Annual Self-Curated Quilt Show, where you decide which of your own creations are worthy to show off to friends and family on blogs and social media, and which ones should be tossed into an active volcano. We have provided for you a handy list of standards and criteria for judging your quilts and quilted items. Please note: research has shown that it is probably best to do your judging on a day where you also have good hair and no chin zits and you are able to button your pants without holding your breath.

Presentation

- Is the quilt pleasing to look at? Does it make you want to do that thing where you shake your booty and pump your fists while chanting short but happy slogans about your personal quilting prowess?
- Is the quilt pleasing to the touch? Do you have to smack people's hands away to keep them from soiling it with their greasy mitts? Or would you have to pay the dog to sleep on it?
- Is it clean enough to photograph in low light with an Instagram filter that is particularly friendly to salsa stains?
- Remember when you had to jot down a phone number on the background fabric with a "disappearing" marker because nobody respects your space and all your pens and paper are never where you left them? Did it disappear? Really? Look closer.
- Are there any loose threads, knots, pet hairs, spiderwebs, rocks, sticks, blood or mysterious crusty places?
- So…how's it hangin'?

Design

- Does it follow the design principles of balance and rhythm? Do you know what those principles are? Do you think they're even real? No, seriously, do you? Because we have no idea.

• Does the binding enhance the overall appearance, or does it just look like you stapled it on and called it a day?

• Are the colors appropriate and pleasing? Because nobody likes baby poop green, even when it's a quilt depicting the wonders of baby poop.

• Is it a quilt depicting the wonders of baby poop? What were you thinking? No. Just no.

• Have you chosen materials appropriate for the design? Do you want to reconsider those repurposed Doritos bags, or are you gonna just go with that and to hell with what anyone thinks?

• Do the colors give the piece movement? If so, are you fast enough to catch it if it gets away?

• Does the backing compliment the colors on the front? Does it say, "Front, you are looking fine today. What say you and me go get a drink and see where this thing goes?"

• Does the backing complement the front? Because apparently that's good, too.

Workmanship

• Do all the points and corners meet? No? Step back ten feet. There you go.

• Are there any holes or incomplete seams? That's why appliqué was invented. Slap on a nice flower and it's all good.

• Does the quilting enhance the design of the patchwork, or does it look like vandalism? Oh, you meant for it to look like that? Well, aren't you artsy?

• If you hid dirty shapes in the stippling, will your mom be able to tell?

• Does it lie flat? If you drape it casually, yet artfully, over a chair or a tree branch, does it solve that little problem? Thought so.

• Finally, is your Photoshopping subtle and non-obvious?

Keep in mind that many of these criteria only count if you are showing your quilts to other quilters. Facebook has post filters that allow you to keep your photos away from anybody except the unwashed masses who think everything you do looks amazing and will praise it even if it's basically just held together with glue and good intentions.

And, most importantly, when judging your own quilts, never take the judge's comments personally. Remember: it's not you, it's…okay, it is you. And that big zit on your chin.

thank you
for calling

I actually like it if I can conduct all of my phone business with an automated system rather than an actual human, particularly if I have to call a fabric store. I was recently in a quilt shop and listened as the sole employee on duty took a phone call from someone who clearly was looking for a particular fabric. The caller had the manufacturer, the name of the designer, the name of the collection, and the name of the print, and the employee said, "None of that helps me; you're just going to have to tell me what it looks like." Those of you who, like me, have worked in a bookstore, will know why I think that is hilarious.

Thank you for calling Quilt Stuff 4 Less, your one-stop shop for all your discount quilting needs. We carry all your favorite fabrics from top designers such as Beulah Frink, Coffee Faucet, Dizzy Mouse, and more! And don't forget—every Tuesday is Coupon Frenzy Day, where you and hundreds of other shoppers compete in grueling tests of patience as you stand in line for hours waiting for the person at the register to find a coupon that actually matches the stuff she wants to buy.

To reach our fabric department, press 1.

(beep)

Thank you for calling the Fabric Department at Quilt Stuff 4 Less. To hear about our specials on Leeway of Lancaster fabrics, press 1. To learn more about our Super Shopper Club card, where you can save up to five percent on fabric purchases over 20 yards (some restrictions apply; discounts may not be used on designer fabrics, premium fabrics, sale fabrics, or fabrics that have any aesthetic appeal whatsoever) for only $99.95 a year, press 2. To cancel your Super Shopper Club Card membership, please go to our website and click on "Customer Service," then "Super Shopper Club," then "Cancel Membership," then, under "Are you sure you wish to cancel," click "yes," and under "Are you really, really sure," click "yes," then fill out the form stating your reasons for cancellation, print, and mail to the corporate office. Please note: envelopes containing death threats will result in an automatic three-year extension of your Super Shopper Club Membership. To speak to the Fabric Department manager, press 3.

(beep)

Hi, thank you for calling. I am either serving customers with a smile or stocking our shelves with even more great fabric bargains for you. I am absolutely not hanging out in the alley behind the store with Sid from Shipping and Receiving, and anybody who says so is a dirty liar. To complain about service you received in the Fabric Department, press 1. To complain about fabric you purchased, press 2. To complain about the sticky spot on the floor near the cutting station that never seems to go away, press 3. To complain about me and Sid, bite me. To speak to the store manager, press 4.

(beep)

Hi, and thank you for calling. I am not available at the moment, either because I am in my court-ordered anger management session, or I am throttling an employee within an inch of her life. Wait. Forget I said that. It's more likely I am working the register because someone didn't show up again, or cutting fabric because someone is up to shenanigans in the alley behind the store with Sid from Shipping and Receiving. Yeah, we all know about it, and no one's jealous, Katy; we're all just kind of grossed out. So, I'm basically trying to do my job plus theirs and I can't be everywhere at once so if you could just lay off and let me do my job in peace then maybe I won't burn this whole place down and you'll still have someplace to shop tomorrow, okay? To leave me a message, press 1. To report shenanigans, press 2. To apply for employment, take a large stick—a good, knobby one—and beat yourself over the head with it. Or press 3. The end result's the same. To inquire about booking a child's birthday party with LuLu the Fiber Clown, press 4.

(beep)

Thank you for calling the Party Department, where we make your birthday boy or girl's day extra special with fun projects using LuLu the Fiber Clown fabrics! All LuLu fabrics have been thoroughly tested on bunnies and monkeys and have been declared "probably safe" by independent labs that are only connected to Quilt Stuff 4 Less by virtue of being owned by the same umbrella corporation, United Petroleum and Hydrocarbons. To book a Party Room, press 1. For instructions on how to remove the LuLu the Fiber Clown fabric dye residue from clothing, upholstery, walls, and children, press 2. To report skin rashes, eyeball swelling, or hallucinations after exposure to LuLu fabrics, press 3. For the legal department, press 4.

(beep)

THANK YOU FOR CALLING THE LEGAL DEPARTMENT. ABANDON ALL HOPE, YE WHO PRESS NUMBERS HERE. TO BE TAKEN THROUGH A LABYRINTHINE MAZE OF OPTIONS AND MESSAGES FOR ALL ETERNITY, PRESS 1. TO SELL US YOUR IMMORTAL SOUL, PRESS 2. TO END THIS CALL, PRESS ZERO.

(beep)

Thank you for calling Quilt Stuff 4 Less, your one-stop shop for all your discount quilting needs! Call us again soon!

the new rules

I sometimes think we also could use an etiquette guide for talking with others on the internet about quilting, but the rules would essentially be, "Be kind to other people about their grammar and spelling," and "If you are compelled by your post topic to say 'if not allowed please delete,' you should probably just not post it."

It has come to our attention that some guild members are forgetting their manners when attending meetings and shows. We therefore offer this guide to new and current members as a gentle reminder that we are not going to take any more of this crap.

General Rules

Please assume that whatever it is you are eyeing with unbridled lust belongs to someone else and should be left alone. Keep your mitts off other members' rotary cutters, mats, fabric, fine jewelry, and attractive relatives unless you are given express permission to do so. "I could tell he wanted me" does not constitute express permission.

Please note that the meeting hall only has five electrical outlets and we all need to share. Just because you snuck in one day and installed a leopard-print outlet cover with "Alma's Plug Spot" painted on it, doesn't mean it's actually your outlet.

Tube tops are not acceptable attire for any guild event. And no, the fact that they are "just mosquito bites" does not allow you an exemption.

Try to keep your questions—about why we are still having a fundraising garage sale when no one ever volunteers for it and we only make a few dollars anyway, and so how come we couldn't consider something more fun, like, say, a car wash or a fashion show or even that Startkicker thingeverybody's doing now, because then all you have to do is make a video and slap it on the internet and people just give you money did you ever think of that huh did you?—as brief as possible.

Please use your cellphones to tweet insults about other members *quietly*.

Show and Tell

Some guild members have been saying there is a three-month waiting period before any new member can present a quilt or quilts at the monthly Show and Tell. This is not true. Once a new member has been through the required hazing process (please see Diane for the date of the next Streak-A-Quilt-Shop/Beer Pong event) he or she is welcome to show a quilt at any time.

Do not shoot spitballs.

Do not make elaborate coughing sounds and then mutter something mean in between the coughs, like "Amateur!" or "Bobbin bimbo!" Everyone can hear you and "bobbin bimbo" is just stupid.

Lectures and Presentations

We are thrilled to see more men joining the quilting world and lately we have had more male quilters give lectures and presentations. Please do not whistle, catcall, or throw underwear at the male speaker. Please do not attempt to slip him your phone number. And please, for goodness sake, do not ask him which way his rotary cutter rolls.

Our speakers are always gracious enough to bring several quilts to show us during their presentations. Please examine your hands closely for chocolate residue before handling our guests' quilts. Mary Ann Jenkins, just don't touch anything, ever. And yes, that includes other quilters.

Our Guild Quilt Show

Our white glove attendants are there for a reason. We know how much you like to fondle the fabric, but many quilts have been soiled from sneaky fingers. Please do not try to bribe the attendants with candy, alcohol, raffle tickets, or Groupons. Please do not try to distract them by shouting, "Fire!" or "Male quilter!"

Please put away your pens, lipsticks, switchblades, and spray paints when looking closely at the quilts.

Shopping carts stolen from the local Target are no longer allowed in the aisles at the quilt show. Please park them in the designated area.

No smoking, drinking, or gambling.

Workshops and Classes

Please note that the karaoke machine has been removed from the classroom area, so there will be no more sing-offs for seat placement.

It is recommended that you arrive to class at least a half hour before the start of class time in order to get set up. Allow one hour if you plan to do a lot of whining.

If you generally spend a large amount of class time telling everyone your method is better, then you should also be prepared to have someone "accidentally" spill a super-size Diet Coke all over your project.

Study your supply list! If your instructor requires you to bring a pan of brownies and an unread copy of *Fifty Shades of Grey*, well then those better darn well be in your bag.

And remember: Check your attitude at the door. You can have it right back as soon as class is over.

letting go

Leah Day, the free-motion quilting guru (www.leahday.com), and one of the people I most admire in the quilting world, often jokes about throwing back a jack and coke before quilting in order to "loosen up" enough to swirl a big ol' quilt under a sewing machine needle. I thought perhaps there might be some other ways to loosen up, and yes we should all be grateful this didn't go to some rather more risqué places because it absolutely could have.

Free motion quilting can be a huge hurdle for today's quilter. We all want to be able to create those fancy, swirling designs on our domestic sewing machines but many of us have no idea how to get started. Some people get through a few, halting stitches and then give up, saying it's just too hard.

Well, I'm here to help. The secret to free motion quilting lies in two words: letting go.

Seriously, try it. What are you holding on to right now? A pencil? A Slurpee? A chinchilla? The mailman? Throw your arms out wide and drop everything. Whoops—okay, go catch the chinchilla and put it back in its cage. There now, don't you feel more free, more open to possibility? Don't worry; the mailman comes back every day.

Now let's examine all the tension you are holding onto in your body. Let your neck relax and your head fall; let all your limbs loosen and feel yourself sinking into a big boneless blob on the floor. Yep, right on the floor. Get on down there. Imagine a giant puddle of flesh. Be the puddle. Did I mention it's probably a good idea to go pee before you do this? No? Oh. Well, now you can really be a puddle.

And while we're on the topic, let's just be frank here. What else are you holding on to in there, hmm? Listen, honey—fiber is a free motion quilter's best friend. A bran muffin a day keeps the longarmer away, that's my motto.

Now that we've freed your physical form of tension and other… stuff, let's move on to all your emotional baggage. Anger, jealousy, fear—just let them all float away on the breeze. Watch them go; that's it. Just like all the money you spent on this non-refundable workshop: gone forever. Bye-bye, sadness! Bye-bye, pain! Forgive all those who have wronged you. Forgive your mom for never approving of any of your boyfriends. Or girlfriends. Forgive your ex for that one time he let your cat out when he came over to fix your sink, and you had to put flyers all over town and that cat never came back and he was just the best cat ever and getting you a new kitten, like, three days later was not the right move at all because nothing could replace Mr. Fluffypants, nothing. Forgive him too. If you can. If not, it's totally understandable.

Now let's turn to more material concerns. Look around your home. See how all your possessions are weighing you down? See how the clutter on your cutting table is a reflection of the clutter in your psyche, in your soul? Just sweep it all away. Maybe into a big bin or something. Look at all your fabrics. You have so many, don't you? Too many. Especially the Tula Pinks. Way too many of those. Just sweep all those into the bin too. And just leave that bin on your front porch and let fate carry it away to a new home, where people appreciate exquisite fabrics and will actually use them instead of hoarding them like, what, are you Gollum or something?

I should probably take a moment to note that all the personal information you were required to supply during sign-up is completely confidential. Don't worry about that at all. Just let it go.

No. No, wait. Don't. Don't do it. DON'T SING THE SONG. Oh, dear. We're singing it.

I'll just wait until everyone is done.

Okay, where were we? Now, we must learn to let go of expectations. See this quilt here? See the feathers and swirls and flowers all artfully stitched upon it? Don't expect to do that. And this one? All geometric, but echoing the quilt blocks themselves, enhancing the design without overpowering it? Yeah, don't expect to do that either. And how about that picture on your phone of a guy with a little bit of a paunch and, let's face it, thinning hair, who you've been dating for, I don't know, freaking eternity? Don't expect an engagement ring out of him. Or employment. Or orgasms. You just release all those expectations into the wind, honey. You'll feel a whole lot better, trust me.

Finally, we must let go of attachments. I bet you never use that ruffler, do you? And who needs a walking foot? We're free motion quilting now; we don't need no stinking walking foot.

Feel how free you are! Your limbs are loose; your heart is open; your mind is ready to access its unlimited potential. Now pull yourself up off the floor, sit at your machine, release your feed dogs—and quilt!

How…uh, how're we doing there? Oh. Oh dear. That didn't go very well, did it? Are you sure you really let everything go? Is there anything else you need to, um, release? Little gas, maybe? No? Crap.

Okay. Here's the real secret: tequila. Just keep a bottle of Cuervo and a shot glass near your machine at all times; two big shots should do it, but if you still feel a little inhibited, go ahead and throw back a couple more. There you go—whoo! Now you feel loose, don't you? Oh okay, yeah, sure, take your top off; we're all friends here. Yeah! We're quilting now, baby! Sure, we're all gonna hate ourselves in the morning, but we don't need to worry about that now! Just let it go! Oh yeah…

LET IT GO. LET IT GOOOO. CAN'T HOLD IT BACK ANY-MOOOOORE!

meet the candidates

When I was a senior in high school, I ran for student body president for some unfathomable reason. I lost, and the person I lost to did the exact same "F-U-N" thing that Ms Halliday does here, and that apparently was the key factor that won over the electorate. Not that I'm still bitter about it or anything.

It's that time of year again! All the positions on the Guild executive council are up for election, and before you ask, yes it has been a whole year since we went through this and, no, we can't just let anarchy reign. So please take a moment and meet the candidates for guild president, and remember: write-in votes are not considered valid and George Clooney probably isn't interested in the job anyway.

1. Marjorie Dornan has been the Hospitality Chairman…Chairperson…Chairist—whatever—for nearly ten years now and thinks it's high time she got to do something else for a change. Do you know what the Hospitality Chairhuman actually does? Greets visitors and new members at the door. Why is this even a thing? No one can actually remember the last time we had a new member and the only visitor Marjorie has ever greeted was the kid who wanted to "catch a Snorlak," whatever that means. Probably something to with drugs.

Marjorie would like everyone to know that she is perfectly capable of handling being president because it can't possibly be that hard. I mean Linda did it, for Pete's sake. Linda herself once said to Marjorie that she could probably spend an entire meeting asleep and snoring like a jackhammer and no one would notice, that's how much attention everybody pays to the president anyway. So, instead of ignoring Marjorie in the back of the room, maybe we could all ignore her at the front of the room for a year. Perhaps then she could actually see the stuff during Show and Tell and not have to rely on Sally Mumford whispering about how ugly they all are to have any idea what's going on.

Vote Marjorie: You People Owe Her

2. Amber Halliday believes that being Guild president is all about F-U-N…FUN! F is for Fresh new ideas. Let's find new ways to raise money, like a car wash or a bake sale! If it works for the PTA (of which

Amber is also president, by the way) it can work for us! U is for Up-
lifting. Let's raise each other up instead of tearing each other down.
Amber proposes a Quilter of the Month award to be given at each
meeting, where the winner gets a tiara and a feather boa and a sparkly
magic wand (all handmade by Amber, of course) and gets to sit in the
Queen Quilter throne for the entire meeting while everyone tells her
how pretty her quilts are and no one is ever allowed to mention the
fact that she uses too much pink. And, lastly, N is for No More Nudity.
This is a quilt guild, not some hippy-dippy art collective, and if Amber
has to see one more nipple on a quilt she will not be happy. Some of us
have children, you know, and they could hear about the nipple when
we go home to tell our spouses how outraged we are by it, and then
they'll join a gang and it'll just be nipples, nipples, nipples. Is that what
we want? Nipple gangs?

Vote Amber: She Knows What's Best For You

3. Jessica Youngchild is a world-famous quilt pattern designer,
fabric designer, YouTube star, and the author of the bestselling book,
Quilting the Jessica Way. Jessica is certain everyone understands this
election is just a formality since she is obviously the only candidate
who has any real accomplishments, but she is willing to go through
the motions to show that she is in touch with common people. Jessica will revitalize the Guild program schedule by bringing in all her
industry friends to do obscenely priced workshops that suit Jessica's
personal aesthetic and/or networking goals. She will also be making
note of any quilts that the rest of the membership are working on, and
if she determines that any of them even remotely resemble something
she once thought of making, she will sue you so hard you'll cry for
your mommy. And if you actually manage to come up with something
original, Jessica may still sue you just because she can. Jessica will do
a book signing at each meeting, with the purchase of a book, or you

can purchase a Fan Package for $130, which includes an autographed book, a photo opportunity, and VIP seating during the Guild meeting. Please remember Jessica does not like to be touched or make eye contact or engage in actual conversation with non-famous people.

Vote Jessica. Now.

4. Roberta Nygard is a quilter, a mom, founder of the Vegan Quilters For Organic Tampons Facebook group, and owner of the GreenOrganicEcoCrafterGoddess Etsy shop. Roberta is committed to making our Guild eco-friendly, sustainable, and ultimately entirely compostable, including the quilts. Far too many non-renewable resources are being used each month at Guild meetings, so Roberta proposes all future meetings be held in the woods and we can all just poop behind a tree. Roberta will also sponsor the creation of a Guild hemp and bamboo farm, with the goal of eventually producing all our own quilting fabric, thread, needles, and snacks. Meetings will be held at dawn so that we can do naked sun salutations while thanking Mother Gaia for her bounty, and Roberta will bring her famous chia kale loaf to share.

Vote Roberta. Preferably while pooping in the woods.

my business plan

When I started selling quilt patterns and other items as well as my books, I decided that I probably ought to have a legitimate business license, and so went about researching everything I needed in order to do that, and I kept coming across the dreaded "business plan" requirement. I could not actually solicit advice from a real human, because that would always be the first question: Have you written your business plan? I think we know what happens when I try to write things that I'm supposed to take seriously.

Executive Summary

The concept of Sip-n-Sew is to provide a quilt shop and cocktail lounge combo in the heart of downtown Springfield. Owner Pauline Provkowski (That's me. Hi!) has over 15 years of experience in quilting and retail sales, and a lifetime of experience with tasty legal intoxicants. Sip-n-Sew will cater to middle-to-upper-class and affluent clientele, though everybody is welcome on Dollar Shot Tuesdays. The quilt shop will specialize in a range of high quality quilting fabric, tools, notions, books and magazines and will offer classes geared for both the experienced quilter (e.g., Advanced Curved Origami Paper Piecing—Blindfolded) and the novice sewist (Meet The Seam Ripper: Your New Best Friend). The adjacent cocktail lounge will provide entertainment for the uninterested spouses of our quilt shop customers, the customers themselves, and the employees of the nearby shipyards.

Sip-n-Sew will leverage Pauline's extensive quilting expertise, as well as the general tendency of everybody in Springfield to tie one on at the slightest provocation, to rapidly gain market share in the competitive quilting supply/dive bar niche. Profitability should be achieved by next Tuesday and first year revenues are expected to be somewhere in the ballpark of a whole hell of a lot.

Objectives

Step 1: Turn Sip-n-Sew into the greatest and most successful quilt shop/gin lover's paradise in all of human history.

Step 2: Grow our customer base to include basically everybody through a combination of savvy marketing and extra-strong margaritas.

Step 3: Profit.

Mission

Sip-n-Sew's mission is to offer our target customers:

• The best quality quilting fabric on the market today, unless we find out that any of our current selection is also being sold at deep discount in someone's Etsy shop, and then we will use it to mop up drink spills.

• A pleasant and welcoming shopping experience, followed by a massive hangover.

• Expert quilting advice and top-shelf tequila.

Market Analysis

The typical quilter in the larger Springfield metro area is between the ages of 22 and 104 (Hi, Grammy!) and has some college education as long as watching TED talks on YouTube counts. These quilters are in need of a local retail establishment where they can purchase quality fabrics and notions while also getting their boogie on to the sick beats of DJ Freaky Fresh Frank on Hip Hop Wednesdays. Research indicates that the typical Springfield quilter will spend an average of $50 per shopping experience if she believes her coupon will work on clearance items, more if she is also throwing back a mojito.

Competition for quilt- and cocktail-savvy customers in the downtown Springfield area include The Quilt Shack—which is literally a shack next door to a Jiffy Lube. There's a flickering neon Open sign that comes on every day, but if you can find anybody who's actually ever been inside there who wasn't serving a subpoena, I'll give you fifty bucks. The other main competitor is Fabric City, over on Highway 89. Sure, their fabrics are cheap, but since you can never find anybody to actually work a register over there, I'm not sure how they're staying in business. Well, unless the company takes a cut of Jeremy Hosner's weed sales in the alley behind the store. And if they don't, they should—that boy's a hustler.

Sales Strategy

The key to Sip-n-Sew's sales strategy is the fact that quilters love to get toasted after a fabric buying binge and tipsy people are more likely to buy multiple yards of Alexander Henry hunks fabric at full retail price. The sales floor of the fabric half of the business will open directly into the bar, providing ample opportunity for patrons of each section to make poor choices in the other. Quilters who purchase over $100 of merchandise in one transaction will be offered a coupon for a free basket of mozzarella sticks and drinkers who pass out in the bathroom will get a free table runner pattern.

Personnel Plan
Sip-n-Sew will have the following staff members:
• Manager
• Assistant manager
• Three retail salespersons
• Four bartenders
• Three to five cocktail waitresses
• And security staff will be provided ad hoc by the local biker gang who will be paid in Budweiser and some of Jeremy Hosner's finest weed—except for Fang, who gets paid in fabric because he loves to make bargello quilts only nobody is supposed to know this so shhhh!

In conclusion, Sip-n-Sew is uniquely positioned to clobber all the competition in the metro Springfield area and to become a beloved hometown institution where the double comfort of handmade quilts and sweet alcohol-induced oblivion come together in one convenient-ly-located shop with ample parking, great selection, and professional enabling.

a cozy retreat

My least favorite feature in any quilting magazine is the profile of a quilter's house. You did not get that pristine, 5-bedroom, palatial modern masterpiece of a house overlooking something vast and scenic on the money you make from quilting, my dear. But I'm so happy for you that you can renew your creativity in your heated pool and do all of your quilting in a room with roughly the same square footage as a high school gymnasium. It's so inspiring!

Nestled on a sunny street leading to a cul-de-sac where the more expensive houses are, the suburban duplex rented by quilter Nancy Martin provides an almost adequate space where she can claw out just a few minutes of quilting time while she attempts to keep her three young boys from routinely dismembering each other. A hand painted sign on the front door reads, "Solicitors Will Be Flayed Alive," hinting at the gentle humor Nancy relies upon to keep her from going freaking insane.

The poop-brown split-level, awkwardly attached to a mirror-image version on the other side, was definitely not Nancy's first choice. "I would have lived basically anywhere but this," Nancy says, "but Clark said this would be just fine because who needs natural light when we have lamps?" Built sometime in the mid-70s by a developer who was eventually jailed for money-laundering his cocaine sales through several contracting businesses, the house is almost exactly the same as every other house on the street, except for those on the aforementioned cul-de-sac, which all have 2 levels and some semblance of a yard. This subtle difference in architecture keeps the neighborhood lively, says Nancy. "Those people won't even speak to us because they have a few more square feet and some grass. I mean, just because you can literally look down on us from the second floor, doesn't mean you're better than us."

With only two bedrooms, one bath, and a partially-finished basement that Nancy's husband Clark has already claimed as his "mancave," the house's diminutive size means that Nancy has to employ her quilter's creativity to find room for 5 people and a sewing machine. She has found herself stitching in her own bedroom, hunched over the coffee table while sitting on the living room sofa, or standing at the kitchen counter—but she finds she can eke out the most precious seconds if she perches the machine on the back of the toilet and straddles the lid. However, this only works, she says, if she manages to get in there "right after Clark has made it essentially uninhabitable for humans who aren't desperate for solitude." Nancy credits several years of diaper blow-outs for her ability to withstand "unholy aromas" and still make a pretty decent churn dash.

Nancy describes her decorating style as "Target clearance rack meets stuff we got free from relatives." Nearly every item in the family's home shows evidence of a handmade touch—from a dent in the side of a particle board bookcase where Clark kicked it when some team or other fumbled a triple play or got put in the penalty kick boxing hole (Nancy isn't quite sure) to the words "Brendon is a stinky poopy face booger head" charmingly written in permanent marker on the headboard of the middle child's bed. A possibly hand-painted sign hanging by the front door reads "In this house we..." with the subsequent lines obscured by a hot pink Post-It note that says "NEED TOILET PAPER."

Wildlife abounds here, Nancy says, "if by 'wildlife' you mean lots of dogs that sit outside and bark all day." Nancy once thought she might have a chance to take over the man-cave when she noticed Clark hadn't been using it for a couple weeks, until she realized he had been avoiding it because of the snake that had taken up residence there. Nancy describes it as "just a rat snake, harmless" while Clark's accounting is more colorful. "That thing was as big around as my arm," he says, thrusting a rather meaty forearm in the air to illustrate. "It had yellow eyes, and I'm pretty sure it had just eaten a cat." Nancy drily notes that were this indeed the case, Clark's responsiveness to a potentially dangerous situation for their young boys was perhaps less than ideal, to which Clark responds, "I had a plan." Meanwhile, Nancy managed to herd the unwanted creature into a bucket, which she then carried outside and dumped in the yard of "the yappiest dog in the neighborhood chorus."

Entertaining is a challenge, Nancy says, since there is no dining room to speak of and the upholstery on all the living room seating has a plethora of mysterious stains. "Even I wonder what I'm sitting on—I don't particularly relish the idea of telling guests that it 'probably' isn't poop. It's just easier if we pretend that we can't have people over because the 'renno' isn't done yet. I don't actually know what it's like to be frustrated with your contractor, but I've been on Facebook enough that I can fake it pretty good."

Nancy finds inspiration for her quilts from the magazines she flips through in the checkout line at the grocery store and from several Facebook quilting groups. "Those groups are the best," Nancy says. "If you ever doubt yourself, just get on one of those and read the posts. People are all like, 'Is it ok if I combine this fluorescent pink camo fabric I found in a dumpster with some of the tinfoil from my anti-alien hat?' And the comments are all, 'Of course you can—it's your quilt!' Trust me, you'll feel better about everything you make." Inspiration also comes from Nancy's three boys, each of whom has a specially-made quilt on his bed. The oldest, Jason, chose a Star Wars theme, while the youngest, Dylan, asked for Minecraft. Brendon, the middle child, apparently had a special request for his quilt. "Boogers," says Nancy. "The boy insisted he wanted a booger quilt." The quilt that resulted is a fascinating array of free-form appliqué blobs in shades of yellow and green that Nancy says "made me question all my life choices" while making it.

Nancy has yet to make a quilt for Clark, however. "He keeps saying if Brendon gets a booger quilt he should get a 'boob quilt.' If he says it one more time, he'll also get a divorce." Nancy's dream is to make a quilt for their bed "big enough that Clark can't possibly yank it all over to his side every night. But I don't know yet if I can free motion something that big on the back of the toilet."

Sometimes, Nancy says wistfully as she picks at something crusty on the arm of the sofa, she looks at those profiles of quilters' homes in magazines and wonders what it must be like to sew in "all that empty space. Does it echo? How do they know if the kids are covering the TV in duct tape when it's that far away?" But she doesn't aspire to own an airy mansion in the country. "It's just three times as much surface area to collect Goldfish crumbs. This place may not be fancy—or, you know, clean—but it's ours, and we can be ourselves here. Until the lease is up, anyway."

quilting reality shows

Any network that wants to talk to me about making any of these shows a reality: I am available for lunch anytime.

Quilting with the Stars

It's season 25, and this year's roster of B-, C-, and even D-list celebrities may be the best yet! Our seasoned sew-pros are teamed up with stars you know and love and struggle to remember, coming together to create weekly challenge quilts, most of which will be dedicated tearfully to a deceased parent or a newborn child. Or a cat. Our stars for this season include That Guy From That One Show, That Woman Who Was On A Late-Night Cable Show A Couple Years Ago, Some Singer Dude, A Middle-Aged Athlete Who Owes A Lot Of Money, A Man Or Woman With A Very Inspiring Story, and Tara Reid.

Kwilting With The Kardashians

The uber-famous Kardashian clan is back and matriarch Kris Jenner has her hands full this season, as all her offspring decide to become famous quilt designers. Even Kanye gets in on the action, producing a runway quilt show during New York Fashion week and insulting Anna Wintour with his choice of bindings. When Taylor Swift enters a quilt into QuiltCon, Kim retaliates by posting numerous nude selfies as well as a recording of a phone call in which Taylor asks Kanye if he thinks dating Tom Hiddleston will increase her chances of getting Best In Show.

Designer House

This is the story of seven quilt pattern designers, picked to live in the same house, and have their lives filmed, to find out what happens when people stop being polite and start getting really snippy about copyright.

Pimp My Machine

Each week, one deserving sewist is selected to have his or her sad, run-down hoopty of a sewing machine tricked out, blinged up, and customized within an inch of its life. Watch as machines held together with duct tape and prayers are transformed into fairy castles, robots, steampunk contraptions, and sergers.

Real Quilters of the Pacific Northwest

The glamorous women and men of the PNW are back for a new season of drama, fun, drinking, and extravagant shopping trips to Fabric Depot. These are the wives and husbands of organic food store tycoons, fair trade bean-to-bar chocolate magnates, and orgasmic hot yoga studio moguls—who all have nothing better to do than sleep with each other's spouses, slap each other silly in locally-owned coffee bars, and take up an insanely expensive hobby.

America's Next Top Quilter

Tyra Banks is back with 14 new quilters all hoping to make it to the finals and win a coveted contract with a top fabric company that pays absolutely nothing but is great exposure. This season, Tyra teaches the quilters all about "smovving"—a technique of smiling with only your wonky, free-form log cabin blocks—as well as "smaper smiecing," "smurved smiecing," "smappliqué," and "smocking."

Stashers

Professional therapists and quilters attempt to help people who compulsively buy fabric, using a combination of cognitive behavioral therapy and more creative hiding places.

Naked and Afraid of Y-Seams

Two complete strangers come together with nothing more than an old Singer treadle machine and some fabric and must complete an entire tumbling blocks quilt—while completely naked. Outfitted with only a Barb's Quilting Hut tote bag, the contestants must acquire fabric, thread, and batting using only their survivalist skills and complete the quilt by the deadline. For season 5, producers have upped the stakes, and will now be tossing live spiders at the contestants just when they get to that part in the y-seam where you have to do the turn-and-flippy thing.

things you need
to stop doing
(to be a better quilter)
by people you know

I'm pretty sure the end of quilting is nigh as I am now starting to see quilting articles and videos with clickbait headlines. Why Quilting Is Completely Stupid and No One Should Do It. You'll Never Guess What I Used To Make All My Quilting Perfect (hint - it's attitude!), and so on. They even usually have Pinterest-ready art for easy saving. And of course it's all semi-ironic.

1 Your Mom

You need to stop slouching for one thing. The good lord gave you a lovely bosom—stop giggling; it's a perfectly innocent word—for a reason: to get a husband. Yes, I know you already have one but I never really liked him so he doesn't count. Also, would some makeup hurt anyone? If you dress up a little, then quilting will feel like a special occasion, won't it? And then maybe you'll start sewing in straight lines and following patterns instead of performing improv comedy or whatever it is you're doing now. You should probably also stop making that gesture at me when I turn my back. I'm pretty sure nice eligible young men don't care for young ladies who "throw the birdie" at their mothers.

2. Your Dad

You should stop using the word "stop." Fortune 500 CEOs all use strategic, forward-thinking words like "bleeding edge" and "pain points". If you're going to conquer the world of quilt business management, you should be doing market research. Have you set up your focus groups? Also, you need a clear business plan. I never even picked a piece of spinach out of my teeth without a business plan, and look at me. And how's your mission statement? What is your vision for the future of this endeavor? What do you mean, it's just a hobby? Don't be ridiculous. Be sure to work on your golf swing—I can't tell you how many deals I made on the golf course. Well, actually, I can. Plenty of time now that I've retired! Let me fix you a scotch and I'll tell you how I closed the Martindale account on the thirteenth hole—hey, where are you going? I don't think that gesture needs to be part of your mission statement, young lady.

3. Your best Instagram friend

You need to stop copying me, okay? Just because I make quilts from free patterns that are basically traditional blocks with white sash-ing, and use fabrics from only one designer because I truly love how much each line looks exactly like the last one, doesn't mean you can do the same thing and not give me credit for inspiring you. And you do it all the time. If I post a picture of my salad, then three weeks later you post a picture of your pizza and you use the exact same filter! Clarendon is my signature filter, and you never acknowledge me when you use it to show off your food! And it hurts; it really hurts. It's bad enough that everybody started taking pictures of stuff on the floor with their toes showing—now my best friend whom I've never actually met in person is just blatantly stealing my work by placing the same orange flower print in the same corner of the same block as me and not thank-ing me for it! Hey! You can't do that. That's MY rude gesture!

4. Your guild frenemy

You need to stop showing off during Show and Tell, because you are making everyone feel bad about themselves and no one wants to quilt anymore because what's the point? Just because you can sew in a sort of straight line doesn't mean the rest of us can, and we know all your almost perfectly matched seams are just your way of telling us we all suck and we do not appreciate it. Every time you stand up there dis-playing something perfectly adequate, I—we, I mean we, every single one of us, not just me—we all just lose our last remaining shreds of self-esteem and have to go write nasty comments on YouTube videos until we feel better. I have taken a very scientific poll of all the people willing to sit next to me and we both—all, all of us, not just me and Gertie—we all agree that your relentless pursuit of competence con-stitutes harassment and creates a toxic environment at guild meetings. We feel that you should withdraw from the guild entirely unless you are willing to start sitting next to me—US—and teach us how to... Hey! That's not fair! I can't get my finger to do that for that long!

5. Your kids

Stop trying to be an autonomous individual with your own needs and look at me. Look at me. Look at me. Mom. Mom. Mom. Mom. Are you looking? Look at me. I CAN DO THAT WITH MY FINGER TOO, MOM—LOOK!

6. Your Significant Other

I don't actually understand what it is you're even doing in there, but does it really have to involve all those sharp things? That round business that can cut off a finger or...other appendages...really seems like overkill to me. I mean, you have scissors. And remember that time you actually sewed right through your finger? Did you really need to show it to me? I'm going to be honest with you: I closed my eyes as much as I could get away with when our children were being born, so I'm not exactly keen to get a close-up of your finger impalement. If you stumble out of there with some sort of pin jammed in your eyeball, that's it. I will die right there in front of you and then who will drive you to the hospital? If you need a hobby, why don't you try pole dancing? Polly's wife does it and she says—aw, geez, is there any blood on that finger??

7. Your Actual Best Friend

You need to stop worrying about what anybody else in the world thinks, because you are a freaking miracle and everything you do is magic. Get off of Instagram, get off of Facebook, get in your sewing room and just create because you are essentially Mister Rogers, Georgia O'Keefe and RuPaul all rolled into one spectacular package. You have amazing hair, an excellent butt, and your quilts are all happiness in cotton form. If I played for the other team I would totally try to seduce you away from your spouse and worship you the rest of our days with my body, and hell, I may do that anyway because you are just that freaking awesome. The way you placed that orange flower print in the corner of that one block was sheer genius, and anybody who can sew through their own finger and laugh about it later probably ought to be ruler of the whole damn universe. Now let's go get a massage and a manicure, because, honey, that beautiful middle finger of yours is looking worn out.

quilt the pounds away

This is probably the only thing I have ever written that one of my kids said they liked. I'm going to call that a win.

Let's face it: quilting is a naturally sedentary activity, and if you quilt all day, you probably aren't getting in all the exercise you need to prevent the dreaded "quilter's butt." But with a little ingenuity you can turn your stitching routine into a fitness routine! We'll show you how you can sneak healthy activities and habits into your usual laziness and sloth, and watch as the pounds melt away! These tips will help you reduce your waistline and your stash!

1. Give yourself "penalty push-ups" every time you have to rip a seam. Either you'll tone up those flabby arms and shoulders or you'll start paying attention to what you're doing for once. Win-win!

2. Fill your house with only messy snacks like Cheetos and powdered sugar doughnuts so you won't be tempted to eat them and get schmutz all over your fabric.

3. Keep your ironing board far away, like across the room, on another floor, or at your mom's house.

4. Do squats while waiting in the cutting counter line at the fabric store. Sure, you'll annoy the other customers and you might get banned if you fart too much, but isn't that a small price to pay for tight glutes?

5. Schedule some walk-and-stitch time with your sewing buddies. Enjoy the great outdoors as you work on your embroidery or English paper piecing project. Studies show that trying not to walk into traffic while stitching is great for your core!

6. Clean your sewing room. I don't know if it burns a lot of calories, but, damn. How do you get any work done in here?

7. Take the farthest parking spot at the quilt shop, even though the

parking lot is basically a small patch of gravel right next to the building that can fit two cars at most and is always completely taken up by that person who drives a Lincoln Continental and somehow manages to park at an angle like she jumped the curb and just landed there. If you can manage to squeeze in next to her, your cardiovascular system will thank you for the five extra steps!

8. Your grandma used a treadle machine but you should be using a treadmill sewing machine. These have not been invented yet, but that's no excuse.

9. Keep yourself accountable by making all your diet and fitness goals public on your blog or Facebook page. Make sure everybody knows exactly how much you weigh now and be sure to post a pic that reveals all your current fat rolls!

10. Turn your guild meetings into fitness boot camps! Your guild buddies may be surprised when you barge up to the front of the room and scream at them to GIVE ME FIFTY, YOU MAGGOTS! But they'll thank you when their delts and pecs are all buff.

11. Use items you already have in your sewing room as fitness equipment. Fun fact: Singer Featherweights are not actually the weight of a feather!

12. Remember to push your water! You can actually use your iron's spray feature to help keep you hydrated during a marathon de-wrinkling sesh. But be careful! You don't want to get it in your eye by mistake.

13. And most important: be positive! Use healthy affirmations when looking in the mirror. Say to yourself, "I am positive I am busting out

of these yoga pants but I absolutely affirm that I will cut a bitch if I have to do another 'penalty push-up' during this quilt project. So I am going to take another hit off my iron and pump some Featherweights until it's time to go yell at some maggots."

my completely original
instagram giveaway

I love Instagram, but the giveaways have gotten out of control. I know most giveaways are really intended to increase reach and gain followers, but I can never bring myself to do those kinds of things. I'll probably never have a career as an "influencer," unless influencing people to read quilt-related writing that has bad words in it counts, and I think it should.

Woo-hoo! I've just reached 14 followers so it's time for a give-away! One lucky winner will receive this partial mini charm pack that I found in the back of a drawer! To be entered to win, you must do ALL the following:

- Follow me.

- Follow @breadandpopsiclestutubean (my bestie).

- Follow @themandudetoolsgrr (my hubby).

- Follow @sexxysadieawyeah (my 11-year-old daughter).

- Unfollow @mom2threesweeties (my former bestie)because she BETRAYED me and totally copied my signature quilting style and my signature filter (Clarendon) and then she gave me the finger and we should all hate her now.

- Repost this picture with the following hashtags:
    - #partialminicharmpackgiveaway
    - #ididntuseallthegoodpiecesjustmostofthem
    - #itonlyhasalittlecathaironit
    - #atleastithinkitscathair
    - #haha

- Post a picture of your current quilting project.

- Post a picture of your cat.

- Of course you have a cat; everybody has at least one cat.

- Seriously?

- Okay, well, post a picture of your tarantula or whatever.

- Go to your local Smoothie Hut and order a large Berry Banana Blaster with peanut butter because it is soooo good, trust me, you'll love it.

- But don't order it with a shot of wheatgrass because that is my signature add-in and you really shouldn't copy people.

- Post a selfie with your smoothie.

- Post a picture of your empty smoothie cup and a sad face emoji.

- Then go through your feed and find any quilts that look even remotely like mine and tag me, giving me credit as your inspiration.

- And if any of them have the Clarendon filter, delete them, you soulless demon.

- Tag at least 100 friends who must all follow me and complete all of the above tasks or your entry will not count.

- I estimate that by the end of this contest I will be followed by everybody in the entire world and when that happens I automatically become supreme ruler of everything (suck it, Beyoncé) and if this does not happen the entire contest is null and void and I will just take my partial charm pack and delete my Instagram account and go try Ello instead.

That's it! Contest is open for 12 weeks and you can enter as often as you want! And please don't copy my signature giveaway style without giving me credit!

a few words about
your quilting
by your dog

Though I wonder whether quilters' cats really love them back, I don't wonder this same thing at all about their dogs. Of course your dog loves you; that's essentially what a dog is—pure, unadulterated, slobbery love.

Well, hello there, human whom I adore above all others. How are you? I must say, you are looking particularly lovely today. Did you do something different with your crotch? It's really quite compelling and I will be pushing my nose into it at every possible opportunity. Oh and hey, I know we were just out there and I did absolutely nothing other than attempt to sniff other people's crotches and then annihilate the Doberman down the road with my frenzied, high-pitched yipping, but I kind of need to go back out. For real this time. No, really. Really. No? We're not going? Well, okay then, but I'm sure you understand that your refusal is a tacit agreement not to yell or make that frowny mad face when the next loud noise causes what we in the canine community like to call a "sudden evacuation event."

I see you are headed into your sewing room, and I of course will follow you in there because 1) I adore you, 2) I have not licked your face nearly enough today, and 3) I assume we will be going in there to play. Now, heretofore we have not done any playing in that room, but I'm sure this is just an oversight on your part and not an organized campaign to prevent all Good Boy Playtime in your personal space. I know you are the wisest creature of us all and so you can obviously see the many wonderful ways we can whoop it up in your special room, but I also know you are very busy doing crucial tasks such as planning my meals, embodying interesting smells, and plotting the demise of that damn Doberman, and so some of these may not have occurred to you lately. Please allow me to enumerate:

1. I can stand near a table and wag my tail so hard that I sweep several things onto the floor, which I will then bark at.

2. I can run at top speed from one end of the room to the other. And, because the room is actually quite small, this will cause me to comically run into all kinds of objects, which I will then bark at.

3. I can put my nose veeeery close to that noisy machine thing that goes up and down while you playfully push me away. (Not as fun because there's not as much barking potential, but still acceptable.)

4. OR—now hear me out on this one—I can go get that tennis ball I found in the gutter and get it nice and slobbery, just the way I like it, and then you can hide it somewhere under all those pretty colorful flat dog beds you keep in there and then I can root around with my wet nose and my claws until I find it! And then we can do it again! And again! Until we pass out or get to go back outside, whichever comes first.

I'm sure you in your infinite wisdom know of several more and I am here to tell you that I am open to any and all suggestions.

And while we are on the subject of the colorful flat dog beds you like to make, I'm afraid we need to have a little chat about the one you are currently working on. Now you know I don't like to complain—unless we're going to the vet and then all bets are off—but I have to admit I am kind of confused about why you would make me a flat dog bed with cats all over it. Cats. You are, of course, the best and smartest human in all the land, but have you been eating strange pills you find in the bathroom trash can like I did that one time and I saw new colors? Perhaps your exceedingly kind and generous nature has blinded you to the realities of the feline personality, which I will enumerate for you here:

1. They are jerks.
2. Such jerks.
3. They will bite your tail when you aren't looking and then jump on your back and ride you around the house while sinking their claws into your flesh like some sort of demon cowboy and when you finally shake them off you're too traumatized to

bark at them properly.

4. And—I'm so sorry to have to tell you this—they do not believe that you are the most wonderful and benevolent human who has ever walked this earth. Can you believe that? They think you are "okay." OKAY. If this is not blasphemy of the highest order I do not know what is, and I must recommend that all felines be banished from this house immediately, including those printed on fabrics that will eventually become my snooze mats.

I of course defer to you in all things but have you considered all of the other design options out there? Perhaps you could acquire fabrics that depict nice slobbery tennis balls or perhaps a glorious array of squeaky toys shaped like human foods I am not actually allowed to eat. Or—now hear me out on this one—perhaps the entire flat dog bed could depict the epic saga of the Good Boy Wonder Dog who was most excellent at fetching balls, barking at things, and giving expert advice to his favorite human. I promise you, if you were to make that, I would chew on it more than anything else in the entire house, including your phone.

I know you are very excited to get on that project right away and I want to encourage you in that endeavor, but first I need to go root around in the kitchen garbage for a quick snack while you take care of our little furry demon problem. Let's meet back here in ten minutes and we can celebrate with tummy rubs and a walk! Yay!

Oh, oops. Never mind on the walk.

have yourself
a quilty little
midwinter festive thing

This is the first year I have actually employed my sewing skills to make teacher gifts for the end of the school year—and quite possibly the last, too.

T is the season, as they say, and no matter what holiday you celebrate this time of year, it probably involves people expecting you to buy them stuff. Holiday commercialism has gotten so out of hand that even the acolytes of the demon Sa'avu are putting aside their usual blood-letting rituals in favor of Secret Sa'avu gift exchanges. And now that the Gaudiest People Who Ever Lived are in power, gift exchanges have gone from "$10 or less" to "$10 or whatever obscene amount you think will most impress people you barely know." Lord only knows what the white supremacists are exchanging this year.

But we are makers, dammit, committed to the principle that if you have to give a gift to That Woman In Accounting Who Keeps An Unusual Amount of Empty Diet Coke Cans In Her Cubicle or to That One Person In Book Club Who Never Reads The Book But Has Lots Of Opinions About It Anyway, then it should be handmade. Here's a handy guide to all the things you could potentially whip out with some fabric and thread that will fulfill all your social obligations and your hard-won sense of identity.

1. **Zipper Pouch.** At best, this is merely 4 pieces of fabric and a zipper, and if you've never sewn a zipper before, what better time to learn than at 11:48 pm on the night before your kid has to bring in a teacher gift or she will JUST DIE. In fact, you know what? Who needs zippers anyway? Zippers are stupid, and frankly, are just the excessive trappings of bourgeois consumerism and so you get a sack. A sack with no way to hold it shut except your own hands BECAUSE SOME PEOPLE NEVER GET ANY CLOSURE, SHEILA.

2. **Infinity scarf.** Because we are all at the age now where we have to make important, daily neck decisions. Instead of wearing itchy turtlenecks that just make your face look fat, you can don a graceful drape of gauzy fabric that will not actually keep you warm but will at least

hide the skin you now realize is starting to look like it's actually melting.

3.   Mug rug. No, Kathy. I will not make you a quilt. You are, quite literally, the most annoying person I have ever met and you make every single meeting a living hell simply by breathing near me. (It's phlegmy, Kathy. So phlegmy.) I'm not going to make you a table runner or a wall hanging—no, I'm going to make you a glorified coaster. Because maybe, just maybe, after you set down the mug of "herbal tea" (Diet Snapple and vodka) you are constantly sipping from, you will then place the wadded up tissue into which you hork up gobs of death slime during staff meetings onto the coaster next to it and not directly on the conference table like some sort of savage. It's a gift for us all, really.

4.   Pillow. Okay, so, I had plans for this, I really did. I found this paper piecing pattern that was George Clooney's face. Like, *Out of Sight, Ocean's Eleven, O Brother Where Art Thou* Clooney. Peak Clooney, in other words. And I thought hey, who wouldn't want to have a fabric representation of an older but wiser Doug Ross to embrace and/or throw at the dog? But then there were all these tiny, tiny parts (charming laugh lines are super difficult to paper piece—who knew?) and it was all so hard to line up, George ended up looking more like Matt Damon and that is just eight million kinds of oh hell no, so I had to burn it and then I ran out of time so I made you this instead. It's purple. Yes, just 2 squares of solid purple sewn together. Shut up—it's your favorite color and you can still throw it at the dog.

5.   Pot holders. For all your acquaintances in Alaska, California, Colorado, Maine, Massachusetts, Nevada, Oregon, and Washington.

6.   Vibrator cozy. Currently, there are no patterns for this in existence (that I know of) other than knitted or crocheted ones, so perhaps some enterprising soul could come up with a design. It would really only need to be four pieces of fabric and a drawstring. In fact, you know what? Who needs drawstrings anyway? Drawstrings are just a symbol of how we are tied down by the patriarchy and so you just get a sack, a sack that you have to hold together with your own hands because we are women and we have to give ourselves our own orgasms SO WE CAN HOLD OUR OWN DAMN SACKS TOGETHER TOO I GUESS, SHEILA.

7. **Gift cards.** It counts if you draw on the envelope.

****

Peace and joy and love to you all, my friends. And Hail Sa'avu.

how pickles make quilting all better

One day, on my Facebook page, I asked for suggestions of topics to write about, and reader Teri suggested "how pickles make quilting all better." That's my kind of challenge right there.

Self-care is so important, isn't it? In the words of our greatest American citizen, RuPaul, how can you love anyone else if you don't love yourself? And loving yourself requires taking care of yourself, and taking care of yourself requires not getting your panties in a twist over some tiny little problem that isn't even important in the grand scheme of things anyway.

But when you are a quilter, your entire existence can be a series of tiny little problems that, added together, become one big problem and now you have an entire row in your guild group quilt that is a WHOLE FOOT shorter than the rest because somebody keeps eyeballing her quarter inch seam and no we can't just tack on some extra fabric at the end, Donna; we may be modern but we're not savages.

So yes, it can be very easy to get your knickers in a wad over many things in quilting, but there is a solution. No, I mean a literal solution of vinegar and water and salt and spices and maybe sugar if you're feeling frisky. I'm talking about, of course, pickles.

That's right, I said pickles. The ancient and venerable arts of pickling and quilting have seen a huge resurgence in recent years, but it is not widely known that the two together can rebalance your waveform energies and positively ionize your neuron pathways. Or something. I don't know for sure—I fell asleep in that TED talk.

Let me give you an example. Let's say you are in your sewing room, just happily quilting along, la dee da la dee da, and suddenly your machine jams up, grinds to a halt, and smoke starts curling out of the motor. And that was the $99 special you got at Kmart because in this freaking economy that's all you can afford and it's not like those tax cuts everybody is all orgasmic over apply to you and now what are you supposed to do? If you're like most quilters, you'll just go lie face down on the floor until the sobbing subsides, but just imagine if you had a jar of pickles next to you at your sewing table. Maybe some sweet gherkins. Then, as you watch your only link to sanity dying in front of you, you can thoughtfully munch on a nice crisp and tangy pickle, feeling your chakras triangulate into a pyramid or something, and when you've finished the entire jar you can hurl it at the machine, effectively venting your frustrations and putting out what might have been an actual fire inside that thing. See? Isn't that better?

Here's another one. Let's say you are at a guild meeting and the guild show chair is handing out assignments but she is a perfectionist micro-managing hell-beast and your assignment—which is basically to stand at the door and hand out flyers—is specific down to the acceptable brand and color of mascara you are allowed to wear, and the chair is all like, "Is there a problem" because your face is pinched in a fit of unspoken rage and it's not like you can say out loud what you're really thinking so you just have to keep it all in to fester like all your unfulfilled dreams. But just imagine if you had a jar of pickles in your hand. Maybe some kosher dills. Then, when the hell-beast is ready to micro-manage your face you can go, "Hoo boy these are some sour pickles—want some?" And when her attention is deflected by the jar of tasty cukes you can run out the door and into sweet, sweet freedom. See? All better.

Really, there's no problem that a good jar or at least a dish of pickles can't solve. In fact, the famous Pickle Dish quilt pattern was so named because Prohibition-era quilters used to keep a small dish of pickles handy to mask the smell of homemade hooch on their breath, since in those days quilting bees were really just speak-easies. And that's where guilds come from, but that's another story for another day.

I hope you'll join me in the long lost tradition of the jar of pickles in the sewing room, because when quilting threatens to get your briefs in a bunch, there's nothing like a bread-n-butter chip to make it all better.

super-helpful
amazon reviews

It's become clear that the reviews on Amazon no longer have any relationship to reality. Both the unqualified praise and the vicious condemnation are now probably authored by someone who was paid to write it, which just goes to show you we can't have nice things anymore. I miss the days when you only had to discern who was a total nutjob and not who got a free hairdryer.

Sew-Rite 6000 Sewing Machine with Extendo-bed
2 out of 5 Stars
I bought this sewing machine because it was the first item that came up when I did a search for "bestest sewing machine ever in the history of the universe" so I trusted that I would be getting a good one. It even has a picture of a country music star on the box, so that was another indicator of quality. I was impressed with how lightweight it was—I mean, why do they make stuff so heavy you have to ask a guy to carry it and then you remember you don't have a guy and then you get all depressed and eat donut holes and write One Direction fan fiction until you pass out? That's not really serving the customer. I also appreciated the inclusion of a box of Sharpies for "personal customization." I drew Harry Styles giving me a foot rub. All in all, this was a pretty great machine.

However, I am only giving it two stars because the country music singer on the box is sleeping with my Harry and I hate her and I hope she dies in a freak sewing machine accident.

Stitch Master plastic bobbins, pack of 100
1 out of 5 stars
WHY ARE THERE SO MANY BOBBINS I ONLY NEED 10 BOBBINS NOT A HUNDRED PLEASE MAKE A SMALLER CONTAINER OF BOBBINS SOME OF US DON'T SEW THAT MUCH YOU KNOW
ALSO THEY SHOULD BE PURPLE. I LOVE PURPLE.
AND CATS

Making Old Quilt Patterns Look Original, by Trudy McQuil-terpants
5 out of 5 stars

I was SO excited when my dear, dear friend Trudy sent me a copy of her new book. Since we are such dear, dear friends, I knew this book would be something special. And boy was I right! This book has it all: lots of pictures of quilts draped across sofas, quilt patterns that have been around since time began but are now totally different because they're, like, way bigger and not brown, and writing that doesn't dare to get too interesting. I hope to be famous someday just like Trudy and I totally don't mind that she stole my idea for this book because now I'm sure she'll let me sit by her in our next guild meeting! Call me, Trudy! Love ya!

6.5-inch square acrylic ruler
4 out of 5 stars
This is a great ruler, but I just got a new pattern and I need 4-inch squares. So now I have to buy a new ruler. They should come in a set of ALL the sizes, not just one. Also, does anybody know where to get purse-shaped rulers?

Blankets-n-Bulges 2015 Calendar
1 out of 5 stars
THEY ARE QUILTS NOT BLANKETS. ALSO BULGES APPARENTLY MEANS MUSCLES NOT WANG. DISAPPOINTED.

A Quilt to Remember, by Lavinia Havisham-Toshington
2 out of 5 stars
Perhaps Miss Havisham-Toshington is unaware of the long, long tradition of quilt-related fiction into which her novel falls, but someone needs to inform her that in this tradition, people simply do NOT do naked, dirty things with each other. I purchased this novel assum-

ing, as anyone would, that I would be reading yet another wholesome account of how a quilt brought together a community or a family and that my heart would be warmed by a tender account of friendship and potluck suppers. Instead, the only thing warmed was an unmentionable place and I feel violated. I did not appreciate being subjected to several long chapters devoted to extremely energetic couplings between Lance, the gorgeous ne'er-do-well farm hand with a shady past, and Sasha, the beautiful eldest daughter of a cruel man who inherits the family farm and vows to show her father that she can grow corn and milk cows and save the land from foreclosure while also lusting after a man she knows she shouldn't want but does anyway. The only reason there's a quilt in the title is because there's an old one in the barn and they keep explicitly fornicating on it instead of quietly going into a bedroom after getting married and then not talking about it like normal people. I had to buy the entire series just to see if they were all as bad and they certainly are. In fact, I have to keep reading them over and over because I honestly can't believe people like this stuff and maybe I'm missing some redeeming aspect of the story, but it's all just bosoms and buns and hay bales. I would have given this zero stars, but I imagine some of those "modern" quilters might like this.

Grip-Tite Finger Covers for Free Motion Quilting
3 out of 5 stars

To be honest, I bought these without really looking at the picture because they were recommended by someone at my guild, who shall remain nameless. (DONNA.) All she said was they were grippy things that go on your fingers to help you hold on to the quilt, but she failed to mention that they are actually super-short condoms. I mean, they don't have a reservoir tip or anything, but they are basically rainjackets for cocktail weenies. I have no idea whether they grip as advertised, because frankly I can't get past my hands looking like some sort of phallic bouquet. And I probably shouldn't mention this, but I threw them in the garbage can and my husband, Chet, found them and accused me of having an affair with our neighbor, Tom, and I can't quite figure out why he singled out Tom but I'm guessing it might have something to do with the size of Tom's, um, tool—and now that I possibly know this I can't face him but he's always out watering his tomatoes and so I can never leave the house again. Plus, HOW WOULD CHET KNOW? So, I'm sure this is a fine product, but I'm docking two stars because I'm pretty sure a quilting notion shouldn't make you question your life choices.

antonio

There was a brief controversy in Quilt Land a couple years ago over the fact that people were sitting on the lap of the representative of a thread company and posting the pics on Instagram and some people felt this was problematic and others lost the remaining shreds of their dignity and got real mad about one individual kinda wondering if that was an okay thing to be doing in this day and age. I say, if you can't sit on the lap of a sexy, European sales representative who occasionally makes somewhat sexist jokes on his personal Twitter account—then whose lap can you sit on? Laps like that were made for sittin' on, am I right?

Hello, sewing lovers. I am Antonio, your hot and sexy fusible interfacing sales representative. I am extra hot because I am from a European country where we find older women who are a little chunky around the middle extremely alluring. Which country, you ask? Does it really matter, darling, as long as I have the funky rrrr's to prove it?

Please allow me to tell you a little bit about our newest fusible interfacing product. We like to call it...Steamy. Steamy is a silky soft interfacing ideal for quilting and appliqué—here, would you like to stroke it? Come on, don't be shy. Let me just lay it across my thigh and you can feel it's remarkable patented softness. Incredible, no? And how do you feel about the interfacing? Oh, that is just my little joke. I am European and we are very friendly, you understand. In my country, touching a man's thigh is a gesture of goodwill and respect. But do not touch my elbow. It doesn't mean anything; I just don't like it.

If Steamy does not bring you the ultimate in fusible pleasure, may I recommend one of our other fine products such as Slinky, the featherweight fusible with a lighter hold. Or, perhaps my personal favorite, Stiffy. Stiffy is perfect for more, shall we say, vigorous applications. A firm hand and a hot iron are all you need to keep Stiffy under control. Stiffy was developed with the adventurous sewist in mind. How about you, darling? Are you adventurous? Would you like to hold my Stiffy? Please, watch the elbow.

In fact, the wonderful (and beautiful, of course) ladies in our testing department have come up with a fantastic project that uses all three interfacing products—a trio, a...what is the word I am looking for? Group? No, that is not quite right. No matter. Still, you must imagine a wonderful party of Steamy, Slinky, and Stiffy all coming together in a magnificent crescendo of creativity. No one goes home from this party unsatisfied, that I can assure you. Because we make excellent fusible products.

Now, we have a very exciting opportunity for you! As you can see over here we have a large bed where we have scattered many packages of fusible interfacing. Isn't that amusing? Many of our customers love to take a picture with me, Antonio, your hot and sexy fusible interfacing representative, so let us make it a photo to treasure forever. Here, I will drape myself artfully across the bed and the fusible interfacing products and you may come lie beside me to gaze into my deep brown eyes as our staff photographer captures the moment on film. Well, on a digital SD card, but it is all the same. There now, are you comfortable? Let me put my arms around you—don't touch my elbow. Ah, darling, you are so lovely. How many pieces would you like to order? We take all major credit cards. And, of course, cash.

the minimalist
quilt studio

Yes, I read Marie Kondo too and I can tell you the whole "does it spark joy" thing obviously doesn't work in a sewing room. It all sparks joy, even the stuff I know I'm never going to use. I love it all anyway and you can take it away from me when you pry it out of my cold, dead hands—unless you're willing to pay me top dollar for my Tula squirrels on Instagram.

We live in an age of acquisitiveness. We have closets and dressers full of clothes that are never worn, collections of knick-knacks that gather dust, and many of us frankly have way too many cats. It's not normal, all those cats. And for those of us who quilt, the desire to obtain, collect, and sometimes lick all the beautiful fabrics that comprise our craft borders on obsession. It certainly doesn't help when fabric manufacturers routinely discontinue our favorite collections, only to release entirely new collections that subsequently become our favorites, until we are so numbed by novelty we stop noticing every single collection now has a deer print for no good reason.

We stuff our shelves with fat quarters and yardage and pre-cuts, most of which will sit for years, never knowing the joy of transforming into a painstakingly made wedding quilt that will eventually be used to line a dog crate. Collecting soon becomes hoarding, especially after we realize Tula Pink squirrel fabric now sells for $80 a yard on Instagram. Perhaps those ferret fabrics you dug out of the bargain bin at JoAnn's will be worth just as much someday, who knows?

But are all those jelly rolls truly making us happy? Are the extra hours our spouses have to work in order to afford the Ikea furniture to store it all really worth it? Does stuffing our underpants to capacity with mini-charm packs really feel as good as we say it does? And just how much yardage can you really lick before you start to cough up fiber-balls? (Hint: It's less than you think.)

What if I were to tell you that there is joy to be found in owning less fabric, in having fewer gadgets, in saying no to yet another pattern? Would you call me crazy? Try to run me out of town on a rail? Do you even know what a rail is or how to get one? No really, I'm asking, do you? It's for a friend.

To help you on your journey towards a simpler sewing life, here are seven ways you can start to de-clutter your studio and begin your new stitching life free from the burdens of too many possessions:

1. Keep track. Take note of every sewing-related purchase you make in a month. How quickly did you run out of paper? How many of those purchases were late-night sales on Instagram for Tula squirrels? Ask yourself this: Are you really in love with pink rodents, or are you just following the latest rodent trend? If naked mole rat fabric starts selling for twenty bucks a fat quarter, are you gonna want that too? Actually, naked mole rat fabric would be pretty cool. But, see, we didn't know that before and now we do.

2. Get rid of duplicates. Just how many Wonder Clips do you really need? When you stop to think about it, do you even need more than one pin? You can just sew until you reach that one, pull it out, and put it in further down. And let's talk about sewing machines, shall we? Be honest—how many do you own? Really? That many? Wow. Okay, well, maybe consider paring those down to just six or seven. Wouldn't want to be hasty.

3. Clear off flat surfaces. Tables, desks, shelves, toilet seats—these are all magnets for clutter. Develop a zero-tolerance policy for storing things on all the flat surfaces in your studio, and you'll find your creativity soaring as you can now probably walk past your cutting table without causing an avalanche. And where should you now keep all the stuff you took off your tables? I bet you have room where some of those sewing machines used to be.

4. Sell what you don't need. When you noted all of your sewing-related spending, you were probably shocked to discover just how much capital you have tied up in squirrels. Get a return on your investment by re-selling those rodents for far more than you paid for them on Instagram. I know several people who have paid for college tuition by selling bags of the lint produced from sewing on Heather Ross Mendocino fabrics. And if you don't have a lot of in-demand and out-of-print fabrics to sell? Just put together a "scrap bundle" full of random pieces with a tiny sliver of some Lizzy House hedgehogs hanging out—people will gladly pay top dollar for just the possibility of some good rodents.

5. Go paperless. Nearly every sewing and quilting book on the market today is also available in an e-book version, so there's no need to cram your shelves full of tree-killing hard copies. Besides, how many quilts have you actually made from any of those books? If you really feel the need to get the full quilt book experience, just read something that makes your eyelids droop and then go look at a churn dash block and call it modern. I promise you, it's exactly the same.

6. Practice mindful sewing. In order to truly appreciate the quilt you are making, you must become one with it. As you sew, honor the fabric by petting it gently, telling it how pretty it is, and assuring it that you love it even if it has no rodents on it. Slow down your machine and time your stitches to your breathing. Breathe in as the needle comes up, out as it descends. Keep a paper bag handy. Engage all your senses while sewing: feel the fabric; see it's beauty; hear the gentle whir of the machine; smell and then taste the weird crusty spot that suddenly appeared in the middle of your block. Maybe it's peanut butter and you could use the protein. Be grateful for this unexpected snack.

7. Remember the reasons you are simplifying. When you're having a hard time letting go of rodents or clearing away nine or ten of your sewing machines, just remember: this isn't about you. This is all about sticking it to that one person in mini-group who thinks she's soooo great just because her sewing room looks like magic elves clean it up every night. Yeah, right. Magic elves from the magic maid service company. Paid for by her magic trust fund.

If you found these tips helpful, be sure to visit our store, quilt-morewithlesscrap.com, to pick up inspirational key chains, ash trays, t-shirts, throat lozenges, office supplies, toothpicks, feminine hygiene products, Lego sets, and novelty ice cube trays.

Made in the USA
Columbia, SC
21 November 2018